THEIR NAME LIVETH

THE BOOK OF THE
SCOTTISH NATIONAL WAR MEMORIAL

THE CASKET IN THE SHRINE

(*Note the motto '* THEIR NAME LIVETH,' *and the Rock itself breaking through the floor*)

THEIR NAME LIVETH

THE BOOK OF THE
SCOTTISH NATIONAL WAR MEMORIAL

BY

IAN HAY

MAJOR JOHN H. BEITH, C.B.E., M.C.

(Late Argyll and Sutherland Highlanders)

WITH TWENTY-TWO ILLUSTRATIONS

LONDON

JOHN LANE THE BODLEY HEAD LIMITED

First published in 1931

Made and Printed in Great Britain
T. and A. Constable Ltd., Printers, Edinburgh

AUTHOR'S NOTE

FOR the benefit of those who are precluded, by conditions of space and circumstance, from visiting the Memorial in person, I have told this story with a fulness of descriptive detail which I fear may prove at once superfluous and inadequate to those who have made the Pilgrimage for themselves. In their case I can but hope that in the years which lie ahead, when actual memories of the place have grown dim—though they can never entirely fade—an occasional reference to these pages may serve to awaken those memories and recapture for a moment the glamour of an unforgettable experience.

ACKNOWLEDGMENT

TO one whose trade is Fiction, the purveying of unadorned Fact is an unfamiliar and arduous business. My grateful thanks, then, are due to the following, for kindly interest in the compilation of this volume, for the provision of facilities, for access to official records, for information upon points of regimental history and tradition, for personal guidance within the Memorial itself, and for time and trouble expended in reading what I have written and verifying its accuracy :—

His Grace The DUKE OF ATHOLL, K.T., Chairman of the S.N.W.M. Committee.

J. WILSON PATERSON, Esq., M.V.O., M.B.E., A.R.I.B.A., etc., Architect to H.M. Office of Works in Scotland.

The Royal Scots Greys.
    Lt.-Colonel A. I. MACDOUGALL, D.S.O., M.C.
    R. TWISLETON-WYKEHAM-FIENNES, Esq.

The Scots Guards.
    Colonel F. G. ALSTON, C.M.G., D.S.O.
    Lt.-Colonel E. W. S. BALFOUR, D.S.O., O.B.E.
    Capt. D. F. WOOLLAN.

CONTENTS

LIST OF ILLUSTRATIONS

The Illustrations in this book are reproduced from copyright photographs by Francis Caird Inglis, Photographer to His Majesty the King at Edinburgh.

THEIR NAME LIVETH

THE BOOK OF THE
SCOTTISH NATIONAL WAR MEMORIAL

CHAPTER I

THE ROAD TO SCOTLAND

FOR the first few years after the War we were all busily employed in putting permanently upon record our pride in our victory and our gratitude to the men who had won it.

Pride was represented by trophies—captured guns and trench mortars, set up on a village green or in front of a municipal building ; or possibly an obsolete British tank, squatting like a large, innocuous toad in a public park for children to swarm over. All this sort of thing was human and inevitable.

Gratitude took a less flamboyant and more endurable form. First the Imperial War Graves Commission embarked upon its pious task of setting in order our military cemeteries upon foreign soil. The result we can see to-day in almost every corner of the known world. There are eight hundred and ninety of these cemeteries in France and Belgium alone. As for the rest of our Dead, they lie in some fifteen thousand known burial places [1]) all over the world, from Dover to Japan, and from Archangel to the Falkland Islands. Most of us, for the best of all reasons, have visited one or more of these; and so long as we live will carry in our hearts the memory of their tidy serenity and wise uniformity—the Stone of Remembrance at one end and the Cross of Sacrifice at the other, with the gleaming white headstones in between, standing row upon row in long serried ranks, like soldiers on parade.

People at home, too, began to realize their responsibility in this matter. Armistice Day ceased to exist as a restaurant orgy: the Two Minutes Silence took its place. The Unknown Warrior was escorted to his grave in Westminster Abbey by the King himself, with Admirals and Field-Marshals walking on foot beside his bier. The era of grateful remembrance had set in. Finally, the Imperial War Museum was

[1] This term includes British War Cemeteries, Military Plots, Civilian Burial Grounds or Cemeteries, and Churchyards and Churchyard Extensions.

opened at the Crystal Palace. It has since been transferred to the Imperial Institute : it would do most of us good to go there once a year, if only to remind ourselves of what we as a people could do then—can do now—by pooling our service and pulling together.

Then the War Memorials began to go up. These were of all kinds, reflecting every phase of emblematic art and patriotic sentiment, from the stark simplicity of the Cenotaph in Whitehall to the spacious symbolism of the Newfoundland Memorial Park in the Somme Valley, with its great stone caribou standing aloft, keeping eternal vigil over the blood-stained heights beyond Thiepval. All over the Empire the Memorials grew, but they grew thickest in England, for the proudest and saddest of all reasons.

Several years have passed. Most of the trophies have gone ; the spirit of the day is against them. But the Memorials remain.

There is no need to visit the War graves in Flanders and Gallipoli to estimate the contribution that England made. Travel to the Border by the Great North Road, and you will see. We choose this route because in this case Scotland happens to be our destination, but almost any other road would do. Every English highway is now one continuous memorial avenue. The cumulative effect upon the traveller's mind is almost unendurable in its poignancy. There they stand—in market places, upon village greens, peeping over churchyard walls, or keeping silent guard over some rural cross-roads. *To the Glory of God*, they usually begin, *and to the Undying Memory*— Then a score, or scores, of names, each of which, gentle or simple, once meant something, perhaps everything, to somebody in that particular township or parish.

As already noted, these local Memorials stand thicker in England than elsewhere. This is natural enough, because England contributed something like seventy-two per cent. of the total casualties of the whole Empire. But there is another reason.

The Englishman does not concern himself overmuch with the affairs of his neighbours. He is proud of his native county ; he holds in affectionate remembrance the village or street where he was born, and the garden or green where he played as a child. But, if he was born in Lancashire, he is not particularly interested, say, in Middlesex, or for that matter in London itself, and *vice versa*. This accounts for the multiplicity of local and intimate War Memorials in England to-day. The county is the unit, not the country.

But Scotland has a different way of ordering these matters, for she is a comparatively small country, small enough to be acutely conscious of herself as a whole. True, she is divided pretty sharply into the Highlands and the Lowlands ; but when it comes to a matter of national feeling, whether you live in Caithness or Galloway, or for that matter in Canada or New Zealand, it is Scotland, Scotland, all the time.

Moreover, Scottish surnames are so few in number and so strongly localized that any Scot can usually tell where another Scot hails from immediately upon hearing his name. In this connection perhaps I may be permitted to quote here certain sentences [1] which were written

[1] From *The First Hundred Thousand.*

during the actual progress of the War—*à propos* of Casualty Lists.

"Englishmen are fond of saying, with the satisfied air of men letting off a really excellent joke, that every one in Scotland knows every one else. As we study this morning's Roll of Honour, we realize that never was a more truthful jest uttered. There is not a Scottish name in the list which is not familiar to us. If we did not know the man—too often the boy—himself, we knew his people, or at least where his home was. In England, if you live in Kent, and you read that the Northumberland Fusiliers have been cut up or the Duke of Cornwall's Light Infantry badly knocked about, you merely sigh that so many more good men should have fallen. Their names are glorious names, but they are only names. But never a Scottish regiment comes under fire but the whole of Scotland feels it. Scotland is small enough to know all her sons by heart. You may live in Berwickshire, and the man who has died may have come from Skye; but his name is quite familiar to you. Big England's mourning is local; little Scotland's is national."

And that perhaps is the reason why Scotland alone among the nations has erected a National War Memorial commemorating in detail the service of every unit of her Arms, and the name of every one of her hundred thousand dead.

It is to visit that Memorial that we have set out upon this journey. So we will now have done with reminiscence, which, whether proud or sorrowful, seems to be inevitable when one or two of the War generation join company. Let us cross the Border at Carter Fell, then follow the winding, undulating North Road, by way of Jedburgh and Soutra Hill, until the silhouette of Arthur's Seat against the northern horizon tells us that the fulfilment of our pilgrimage is at hand.

CHAPTER II

THE OPENING SCENE

OBVIOUSLY, the place for a country's national Memorial must be its capital city. This being conceded, where in Edinburgh could the Memorial most appropriately stand ? This was a difficult question to answer, for Edinburgh, whose Old Town is one of the most picturesque, as its New Town is one of the most beautiful cities in the world, offered a multiplicity of sites ideal for the purpose.

As we know, the discussion upon this point was long and thorough, as was only fitting. Many things had to be considered—a convenient and accessible situation, spaciousness of outlook, and above all an appropriate setting— in other words, all that is summed up to every good Scot in the mystic word "amenity". Upon such historic ground as Edinburgh almost any site would have been appropriate, but it was felt that this had to be the site of sites. Deep and

EDINBURGH CASTLE, FROM THE EAST

anxious were the consultations. Skylines were
tested, experimental structures run up. The
exact form and scope of the Memorial itself
were the subject of long and even heated debate.
The public mind changed more than once, as
fresh arguments were brought to bear.

In the end the summit of the Castle Rock was
selected as the site of the Memorial. It was a
bold decision, for the objections were obvious
and formidable. First of all ranked the question
of accessibility. The Memorial was intended to
be the tryst of the living as well as a monument
to the dead. How many people would trouble
to toil up the Mound, the Lawnmarket, and
Castle Hill, then traverse the wind-swept Esplanade and breast the cobbled roadway which
winds up and up through the Inner Barrier,
through the Portcullis Gate, past the Six Gun
Battery, through Foog's Gate, to the level of
Mons Meg herself, all to visit a modern building
of unspecified design, which—and here came
objection number two—might prove itself an
eyesore and excrescence upon the ancient, digni-
fied, and time-worn fabric of the Castle. For, if

this edifice turned out a failure, that failure would be the most conspicuous thing in Scotland.

These were justifiable misgivings and legitimate queries. Time has answered them both. The people of Scotland are apparently quite accustomed to scaling heights : already in three years countless thousands of them have visited the Memorial, and even to-day the place is sometimes thronged from opening-time till dusk. On public holidays patient queues some four hundred yards long have been known, after lining Crown Square, to stretch down the winding road as far as the New Barracks. In the early days they sometimes extended to the foot of the Esplanade.

As for the amenity of the Castle Rock, the Architect and the group of men and women who designed the Memorial, and the craftsmen and builders who brought those designs into effect, have among them created something of which the world for once can say—and has said, in no uncertain voice :—" This is perfect."

The original plan, it is interesting to note, was not executed. The erection of an entirely new building upon the Rock, however beautiful the structure, would have involved a material alteration in the historic and familiar skyline of the Castle. Public opinion was very strong against the change. The Committee met the difficulty by suggesting the conversion of an existing building ; and the Architect expressed himself willing to remodel his plans to accommodate a perfectly natural expression of popular sentiment. Fortunately the very structure was standing ready to his hand.

On the summit of the Rock, on the edge of the cliff which drops almost sheer down to the Grassmarket on the south side, stands Palace Yard, or Crown Square, a grey and historic quadrangle about a hundred feet across. The southern edge is occupied by the ancient Banqueting Hall, the scene of many a royal revel and one monstrous breach of faith and hospitality ; for it was from here, in 1440, that the great Earl of Douglas and his younger brother were dragged to their death from the board of the ten-year-old boy king, James II, whither they had been lured by Crichton and Livingstone.

Below and adjacent are casemates and dungeons, where innumerable captives have languished— Montrose, the two Argylls, each in his turn, and a host of French prisoners of war of the Napoleonic era.

Along the west side of the Yard runs a low building of no particular historic importance— it is now being converted, most appropriately, into a Military Museum—but on the east, looking down upon the Old Town, stands the Palace Block, in whose grey stones Scottish history is written deep and indelibly. In a little dark room at the south end of it Mary Queen of Scots gave birth to King James—the Sixth of Scotland and the First of England. In the centre, just under the Crown Room Tower, in the stone-vaulted Crown Chamber, are displayed the Scottish Regalia and other royal jewels—the so-called Honours of Scotland. They have not always been so visible or so secure. After the Battle of Dunbar they were sent to Dunnottar Castle, for safe keeping from Cromwell. Thereafter they lay buried for ten years beneath the floor of the Parish Church of Kinneff, until

Charles II came to his own again. Again, in 1707, after the Union, to save them from being sent to England they were securely sealed up in a chest in the Crown Chamber itself, and lay almost forgotten for more than a hundred years. Sir Walter Scott discovered them, and they were restored, mainly by his efforts, to their former state and dignity. During the Great War they were removed once more, this time to one of the ancient vaults beneath the ground floor of the Palace ; and not without reason, for in 1916 a Zeppelin dropped a bomb upon the Rock itself, leaving a lasting scar upon its venerable face.

On this spot, then, the very centre and focus of so many Scottish traditions and memories, it was decided to erect the National War Memorial. And on the fourth side of the Yard was found not only a worthy site but the elements of a suitable edifice. This was the so-called Billings' Building, which had served mainly, during the hundred and fifty odd years of its existence, as barrack accommodation. With the removal, seven years ago, of the greater part of the garrison to the less spectacular but infinitely more habitable new barracks at Redford, a few miles away, Billings' Building fell into disuse. But for all its prosaic record, it covered historic ground. Here once stood the Chapel of St Mary, founded by King David I, and restored by King David II about the middle of the fourteenth century. Moreover, the Building itself was of good seasoned stone, which would serve, as it were, to dilute the new material and save the Memorial from all appearance of aggressive modernity.

So the happy choice was made, and presently confirmed by the King and his Ministers. A Charter was added, making the official blessing perpetual. The Committee, with the Prince of Wales as President and the Duke of Atholl as Chairman, announced their decision to the country, and appealed for funds. These poured in from all parts of Scotland—Scotland Domestic and Scotland Overseas—and presently Sir Robert Lorimer, the Architect-in-Chief, was bidden, with his partner, Mr. John F. Matthew, and chosen band of craftsmen, to set to work. Some two hundred artists, artificers, and labourers participated in all. You will find the names of those chiefly responsible set out at the end of this volume. They could be mentioned here in greater prominence ; but it was, and still is, their common desire that your attention should go to the work and not to the workers.

And so the Memorial went up, "built by Scottish brains, Scottish hands, and Scottish money."[1] The idea was first suggested in 1917, and the Opening Ceremony took place, just ten years later, upon July 14th, 1927.

II

Probably the very best view of the proceedings upon that lovely and memorable morning was vouchsafed to certain representatives of the B.B.C., who were stationed upon the summit of

---

[1] The first subscription actually received was one of five hundred pounds from a prominent man of business. The second was half-a-crown, sent by an ex-tinker serving with the Black Watch in France.

the flag-tower, looking right down into the
Square itself, for the purpose of conveying to
brother Scots the world over, by means of the
newest marvel of modern science, some im-
pression, however inadequate, of the historic
scene below. And this is what they saw.

Beneath their eyes lay Crown Square, occupied by the Guard of Honour—a platoon of
the Second Cameron Highlanders, with de-
tachments from the Navy and Air Force, who
stood facing the newly completed Memorial—
together with the Colour Parties and all those
officially concerned with the ceremony. The
actual spectators were all outside the Yard :
there was no room for them anywhere else. The
most fortunate of these occupied a stand adjacent to the Half Moon Battery, which is built
upon the summit of what was once David's
Tower, the strongest defensive post in the whole
Castle, now buried and hidden in a later ex-
tension of the Castle fortifications. For three
and a half centuries the Half Moon Battery has
frowned down upon the High Street and the
sometimes recalcitrant Parliament House; but

the only voice now heard from its embrasures is that of the familiar one o'clock gun.

The stand was so placed as to look right into the Square, through the lofty arch in its north-eastern corner. The rest of the spectators were distributed, upon platforms, or chairs, or their own feet, all down the steep cobbled road which winds from the summit of the Rock, through barrack yards and under frowning arches, to the great Esplanade outside the drawbridge, the old parade-ground of the garrison.

It was down on the Esplanade that the real crowds were seen to be gathered, for it was by this route that the Prince—and later their Majesties—must pass upon their way to the Opening Ceremony. Beyond the Esplanade, overflowing down the beflagged Royal Mile, past St Giles' and the Parliament House, along High Street and the Canongate, as far as Holy-rood itself, stretched more crowds—eager, expectant, but curiously restrained. Here was a public festival with a Sabbath atmosphere.

The day had dawned still and misty, but just before the appointed hour the sun broke through, and the watchers on the tower had some opportunity to realize the grandeur of the setting in which the Memorial was to stand during the centuries to come.

To the east stood Arthur's Seat and Salisbury Crags, slowly emerging from the mist, and over-topping the Castle Rock itself. To the west rose the low, wooded ridge of Corstorphine Hill, with its familiar monument on top, and the Forth Bridge, rendered as delicate as tracery by the hazy distance, peeping over its shoulder. To left and right of the Hill ran the white ribbons of the Glasgow and Queensferry Roads. Further away the red slag-heaps of Broxburn stood up against the blue sky. Further away still a faint lofty blur was visible—some outpost of the Grampians. Ben Ledi, perhaps.

To the south rose the Pentlands, with the green farmlands of Midlothian lapping in waves round their feet, and the white plume of the London morning express plainly visible, as it puffed valiantly on its way up the stiff gradient to Midcalder and Cobbinshaw.

But naturally it was to the north that the eye

was chiefly attracted, for there, three hundred
feet below, lay the noble panorama of Princes
Street and its Gardens, gay with flags and
flowers and alive with people ; then, rising from
the valley, the stately prospect of the New Town,
with its gleaming domes and spires. Beyond that,
the waters of the widening Forth, Inchkeith,
Inchcolm, and the green hills of Fife.

Meanwhile, things were beginning to stir
down in Crown Square. Representatives and
guests of honour were arriving : nearly every
notability in Scotland seemed to be present :
every face was familiar. There was an in-
triguing variety of uniforms and vestments.
The Lyon King of Arms was there, resplendent
in red and gold, with his Heralds and Pursui-
vants. In one corner stood the Lord-Lieu-
tenants of Scotland, in another a group of legal
and civic dignitaries. The cassocks of the St
Giles' Choir made a purple splash against the
grey stonework of the Memorial itself. Upon
the steps before the doorway stood the official
clergy in their flowing robes—the three
Moderators and the Primus. But in the main,

and rightly, it was the day of the Soldiers, and of the women who had helped them. There stood Earl Haig himself, in his service uniform and Balmoral bonnet, waiting inconspicuously amid a notable group of officers. The Duke of Atholl, who to-day, after years of selfless toil, was to see the crown of achievement set upon his labours, wore the uniform of the Scottish Horse, his Duchess that of the Red Cross. The Secretary of State for Scotland, Sir John Gilmour, wore service dress too. Princess Mary, when she arrived, was seen to be wearing the simple blue uniform of a V.A.D.

But now the appointed hour was approaching. The sound of the Hundred and Twenty-First Psalm, which had for some time been rolling up from the Esplanade, died away, and silence fell. A closed motor-car was seen approaching from the High Street. Here was the Prince of Wales, come to perform the Opening Ceremony.

The car slid across the drawbridge, and disappeared in the maze of buildings at the base of the Rock. A few minutes later it emerged near the summit, climbing the steep curve which runs through what was once the Governor's Garden, and terminates beside the tiny, eight-hundred-year-old Chapel of St Margaret, with Mons Meg keeping proud and stately guard close by. It stopped, between Half Moon Battery and the arched entrance to Crown Yard; an order rang out, the Guard of Honour came to attention with a resonant clash; the Colours dipped low. The figures of eager, interested spectators—a chosen few—appeared upon the roof of the Banqueting Hall and in the windows surrounding the Yard. Behind them, in the dim recesses of those historic chambers, it was not difficult to imagine other figures—shadowy forms in crown and robe, in cloak and doublet, in farthingale and ruff—Robert the Bruce, Montrose, Argyll, John Knox, and a hundred others; even gay, hapless, tragic Mary herself—all peering down over modern and material shoulders at the strange yet familiar scene of pageantry below.

The ceremony was studiously simple. The slight, familiar figure, in the service uniform and diced glengarry of the Royal Scots Fusiliers,

mounted the flight of steps leading to the
entrance, turned to face the Guard of Honour,
and stood rigidly at the salute as the National
Anthem rolled forth.

Then followed the brief Service of Dedication
by the three Moderators ; after which the Prince
turned again and approached the stout oaken
doors of the Memorial. He placed a golden
key in the lock, and the doors opened. The
sound of those royal footsteps, and the turning
of that key, were faithfully conveyed by a cunningly placed microphone to the ears of in-
visible thousands all over the Empire.

Next, to the singing of *Scots wha hae*, the
Colour Party filed slowly across the Yard,
dipping their Colours as they reached the door,
and disappeared within. It was not fortuitously
that the entrance to the Memorial was made
small in comparison with the main bulk of the
building. There is no actual need to bow the
head in order to pass through the door (as is the
case in the Church of the Nativity at Bethlehem),
but that low arch undoubtedly serves as a reminder to the spirit. Certainly no one who saw

those Colours dip to enter will ever forget the reverence of the scene.

The Prince now passed from view into the Memorial, to take his stand beside the open Casket within the Shrine. He was followed by a stately procession of Colonels Commandant and other high representatives, bearing those Rolls upon which are commemorated the names of the hundred thousand Scottish men and women who died for King and Country. Earl Haig himself bore the Roll of the King's Own Scottish Borderers; Lord Horne that of the Royal Regiment of Artillery; Sir Ian Hamilton that of the Gordons; the Duchess of Atholl that of the Women's Services. All this to the moving strains of *The Flowers of the Forest*.

The procession disappeared. A brief pause followed, while within the Shrine the Prince received the Rolls and deposited them in the Casket—all save four, reserved for the King and Queen.[1] Presently the voice of the Primus was

---

[1] These were the Rolls of the Royal Navy, the Royal Scots Greys, the Royal Air Force, and the Women's Services. One of the latter was also deposited by Princess Mary.

heard uplifted in the Benediction. In Crown Yard the band crashed out again into the National Anthem. Then came Last Post. Another brief, tense pause, and *Réveillé* rang out, sweet and true. The Ceremony of Dedication was ended.

Nothing now remained but to await the arrival of the first official visitors to the Memorial—the King and Queen and Princess Mary. And on the stroke of noon, while the clocks of Edinburgh were still chiming, the royal car rolled into the Yard. Their Majesties alighted. They mounted the steps; a little group of notabilities followed, and the party disappeared within. After half an hour they emerged again. The National Shrine had been royally visited and royally approved. It was now ready for its people.

THE EXTERIOR, FROM CROWN SQUARE

CHAPTER III

THE EXTERIOR WALLS

TO appreciate the exterior and general outline of the Memorial building we cannot
do better than climb once more to the top
of the flag-tower and look down into Crown
Square.

In shape the Memorial resembles a broad,
thick capital E turned on its side, with its three
arms pointing southward into the Yard.   From
the north side—the back of the E as it were—
projects a semi-circular building, or apse.   This
contains the Shrine, which we shall visit last of
all.   Meanwhile, let us survey the front of the
Memorial.

The porch, or entrance, is set in the end of
the short centre arm of the E, and is approached
by a semi-circular flight of shallow steps guarded
on either side by the Unicorn and the Lion.
The other two arms form bays in the main
building, or Hall of Honour.   The roof is flat.

The first thing we notice is that the body of the Memorial is composed of slightly darker stone than its projections. This is natural enough, for the porch and bays are composed mainly of new stone, brought from Doddington Quarry, in Northumberland ; but so cunningly have the old and the new been graded and blended that no actual junction or dividing line is perceptible. In due course the hand of time will efface these slight differences altogether.

Before we go further in our detailed scrutiny, let us pause and ask ourselves two questions. Firstly, what were the ideas—the ideals—which the designers of the Memorial had to symbolize and embody in their creation ? Secondly, what were the limits—the limitations—within which they were constrained to work ?

The second question shall be answered first They had to remember all the time that they were building something for *Scotland*—a land of certain definite and jealously guarded ecclesiastical traditions. This meant that they were committed to a design which precluded anything in the shape of ritualistic suggestion or

THE EXTERIOR, SHOWING THE BACK OF THE SHRINE

exotic adornment. Perhaps this was no bad thing, for it implied in itself a scheme of rugged simplicity. At the same time it permitted the occasional employment of the secular touch, without offence to or detraction from the sacred character of the Memorial as a whole.

With this in mind, we can answer the first question more easily. What, within these limits, was the scope and purpose of the Memorial? Firstly, the provision of an official and historic record of Scotland's War Service; secondly, the expression of Scotland's sorrow for her dead, her pride in their achievement, and her profound faith in the ultimate good of their sacrifice. In other words, all that is summed up in the simple inscription cut deep above the keystone of the central arch of the doorway :—

To the Glory of God,
And In Memory of Scots Who Fell, 1914-1918.

The first of these objects—historical completeness—justifies, and occasionally necessitates, a certain secularity of treatment. This fact is immediately apparent in some of the external adornments of the Memorial—sundry strange cabalistic signs and totems.   These have an interesting significance for the average Scottish infantry soldier.

In the early days of the War, after the old Expeditionary Force had been developed to its full establishment of seven Divisions—and if you wish to be reminded of what they did, read Lord Ernest Hamilton's book upon the subject [1] —the Divisions of the New Armies had allotted to them sundry numbers and designations ; and the lower the number the prouder the Division, as being nearer to the immortal parent body. Ultimately there were more than seventy of these Divisions.   The numbers with which the Scottish infantry soldier was chiefly concerned were Nine, Fifteen, Fifty-One, and Fifty-Two. The Ninth and Fifteenth were two of the earliest Kitchener Divisions—in fact, the Ninth was the very first Division of the New Army— while the Fifty-First and Fifty-Second were the famous Highland and Lowland Territorial Divisions.

However, when the War had been in progress

[1] *The First Seven Divisions*, by Lord Ernest Hamilton.

for considerably more than a year, the powers above realized that to advertise your numerical strength to the enemy and his spies is not always the highest wisdom. So the cherished numbers were painted out from Divisional Artillery limbers and Infantry Transport waggons, and badges or totems took their place. Some of these were symbolic, some utilitarian, and some frankly humorous. Those allotted to the Scottish Divisions were admirable and appropriate of their kind. We shall see them all, reproduced in stone, when we descend from our eyrie and examine the exterior of the Memorial. Meanwhile, upon the front wall we note the more orthodox badges of the Royal Army Medical Corps and Royal Air Force.

So much for the secular touch. But the message conveyed by the façade of the building as a whole is in the main, and most properly, of a symbolic and spiritual character. And there is not a carving or figure upon it which has not a meaning and significance of its own. We shall speedily recognize this fact when we come to make the circuit of the outer walls. We shall note that the wreaths surrounding the badges of the various Services are of different kinds. The Navy has oak, for Britain, and laurel, for victory. The Army has laurel ; the Royal Air Force has rowan, which grows in the open and high places. The Women's Corps has roses and lilies, for sweetness and purity.

Take the symbolism, again, of the animal figures which you will observe on the capitals of the windows. These represent the Vices, in contrast to the Virtues, which are contained in the niches. Note for instance the Vice of Self-Indulgence, represented by the Antelope, which, intent upon the pleasures of this world, browses upon luscious leaves, heedless of the two leopards waiting to devour it.

Let us descend to Crown Court, and approach the Memorial. The arched doorway itself is set within a greater and much loftier arch. In a deep recess above the one arch and below the other hovers a mystic figure, representing the Survival of the Spirit : it rises from the ashes of the Phœnix, the age-long emblem of Immortality. However bright the noonday sun, the

Face, deeply retired within the arch, is always in shadow. Other symbolic figures are enshrined in niches upon the front of the Memorial: blindfold Justice, Mercy, Peace, Courage. The figure of Mercy, a warrior in armour protecting a child, is particularly striking. Below these, on either side of the porch, runs a broad terrace where pilgrims may lay, or hang, their votive offering of memorial wreaths. It is seldom undecorated.

Now we pass from Crown Square, through a narrow opening in the north-west corner, and examine the west wall. This is chiefly occupied by the two western windows of the Hall of Honour, which we shall presently study from within; but between the windows you may observe another symbolic figure—Freedom, casting away a chain. There are two more badges here—of the Royal Naval Reserve and the Women's Services.

On the north side, where the buttressed apse of the Shrine juts out, we have an opportunity to appreciate how completely the projectors of the Memorial have succeeded in setting their work upon the very pinnacle of things ; for here the ancient Rock itself, its fissures and crannies carpeted with grass and lichen, forms the visible foundation of the Memorial. Its actual summit we shall see within.

At the end of the apse, between the two most northerly buttresses and above the centre window, you may note Scotland's patron saint, Saint Andrew, the Fisher of Men, casting away his nets to follow the Master. On the wall to the right are the totems of the Ninth and Fifteenth Divisions, appropriately adjacent to one another, for these two famous units fought their first battle almost side by side, at Loos, in September, 1915. The badge of the Ninth Division is a thistle—it was green, on a white ground—that of the Fifteenth a triangle set within a circle. These two are balanced, on the left, by the badges of the Fifty-First, the Highland Division, a monogram presenting the letters H.D. in the form of a cipher, and the Fifty-Second, Lowland, which displays a thistle set in the centre of a St Andrew's Cross, the whole being contained in the angle of a capital L.

Between the totems of the Ninth and Fifteenth is set the figure of Truth, between that of the Fifty-First and Fifty-Second, the figure of Charity.

Now we pass round to the east side. Here are two other windows. Between them stands the figure of Knowledge—appropriately enough after those years of fierce and memorable education.

On either side of these windows are set the badges of the Navy and Army—the Old Regulars. And here let us pause to consider what the second of these badges means to Scotland as a whole. In our affectionate remembrance of those sons and brothers of ours who flocked so readily to the Colours when the call came, let us see to it that we do not overlook those who were there already—who had long since dedicated themselves to this Service, and were now waiting, ready and willing, at a time when all were willing but few were ready, to stand up to the first rush and cover with their own bodies the critical period of national preparation. There are very very few of them left now, but let us never forget who they were and what they did.

c

What they did, so far as Scotland is concerned, the Roll of Honour inside the Memorial will tell us. Who they were can be briefly set down here. They were the Royal Scots Greys, the Scots Guards, and the ten regular Scottish regiments of the Line—the Royal Scots, the Royal Scots Fusiliers, the King's Own Scottish Borderers, the Scottish Rifles (Cameronians), the Black Watch, the Highland Light Infantry, the Seaforth Highlanders, the Gordon Highlanders, the Cameron Highlanders, and the Argyll and Sutherland Highlanders. These ten were the parents of the innumerable Service battalions which made up the new Scottish Divisions. The Royal Scots headed the list, with no less than thirty-five such lusty sons.

That is what this inconspicuous stone badge commemorates, set up on the eastern outer wall of the Shrine—the example, the service, and the sacrifice of the Old Regulars.

The circuit of the exterior walls is completed. Let us pass within.

CHAPTER IV

THE HALL OF HONOUR

SO far all that we have seen of the Memorial is a rugged four-square edifice of stone, with step-ended gables, set upon a rock and lifting its grey face to the wind and rain of a northern climate. It might be some feudal keep crowning a lonely Scottish hill-top. The more stunning, then, is the marvel of the contrast when we pass through the arch of the doorway and find ourselves within. We have entered a fortress to find ourselves in a sanctuary. Here is nothing but calm, luminous, cloistered serenity —mystic—wonderful—and the hush of everlasting peace—a long vista of richly-tinted windows, of gleaming stone and glowing bronze, of Regimental Colours, of eye-arresting inscriptions and texts.

But we must not anticipate. Let us inaugurate our pilgrimage in due form, beginning with the porchway itself. The very doors arrest our attention. They are of stout Scottish oak, braced with wrought-iron hinges, and evidently quite determined to last as long as the treasures they guard.

Within the porch, carved above the lintel of the inner doorway, we observe the Pelican of the Wilderness, feeding her young with blood from her own heart—a most faithful and moving symbol to set at the entrance of this temple of sacrifice. Three familiar, but none the less appropriate words of Kipling, *Lest We Forget*, set underneath, serve to emphasize the message.

The porch is lighted by two small windows, one on either side. That on the left presents the arms of Scotland previous to the Union of 1707, that on the right the arms of the present day. Under the first are carved the familiar lines from the Hundred and Twenty-Fourth Psalm :—*Our soul is escaped even as a bird out of the snare of the fowler : the snare is broken and we are delivered ;* under the second :—*Our help standeth in the name of the Lord, who hath made heaven and earth.* In the low roof a centre boss depicts an angel raising a human soul from the

THE HALL OF HONOUR
(Looking west, towards Royal Air Force Window)

deep waters of affliction. *Out of the depths have
I cried unto Thee.*

Upon a bench beside us stands a large iron-
bound box, into which those who pass may cast
what offering they will. Sometimes, on public
holidays, that box is filled in half a day—chiefly
with coins of humble denomination, for few of
our pilgrims are rich in this world's goods ; but
filled none the less. The widow's mite.[1]

And now we pass through a second doorway
and are within the body of the Memorial itself—
in the Hall of Honour, which stretches away to
east and west of us. Upon its north side, exactly opposite, stands the Shrine, entered by a
lofty narrow arch and guarded by gates of
wrought iron. We shall defer that visit until
the end.

And now the marvel of contrast already mentioned breaks upon us. From without, the

[1] The sums so collected are devoted partly to the general
cost of upkeep, partly to the expenses connected with the
holding of an annual memorial parade, and partly to the
equipping of the new Military Memorial Museum which,
under the supervision of Major Mackay Scobie, is now being
established on the west side of Crown Square. Admission
to the War Memorial itself is of course free.

Memorial appeared square, stocky, and grey. Here within it is long, ethereal, and luminous, with the vaulted roof of a basilica. The roof is supported on either side by a row of octagonal columns with bold capitals, set close against the wall and forming a little bay between each pair. The purpose of these bays we shall discover presently. The floor is of polished green granite, from Ailsa Craig. The interior stone of the Memorial itself came from a Scottish quarry— Swinton, in Berwickshire. The windows are of stained glass—not the deep, rich tints so familiar in English ecclesiastical architecture ; for this might create too dark an atmosphere, and the whole keynote of this hall of remembrance is light, and more light. The prevailing colour is a bluish grey, like a Scottish sea and sky in summer weather.

What else do we observe in our first swift survey ? Regimental Colours, gleaming everywhere against white stone—those Colours which were borne here so reverently upon the Day of Dedication. Most conspicuous of all, running right round the building above the tops of the columns, a continuous frieze of battle names, cut in great capital letters. What memories they recall. Mons and Le Cateau, where the Old Regulars, completely isolated by the unadvertised retirement of their Allies on the right, fought the greatest rear-guard action in our history since Sir John Moore's retreat to Corunna. Ypres, for four long years the grave of British soldiers and of German hopes, ever memorable for the First Battle, wherein three weary Divisions, stretched out into an attenuated line, with not another man or gun left between them and the Channel ports, fighting against odds of eight to one, brought the enemy to a final standstill and stabilized the line from the sea to the Alps. (Scotland played her part, and more, in that tremendous encounter : the First Camerons and Second Royal Scots Fusiliers, in accomplishing their given task, were practically obliterated.) Gallipoli, where, on the glorious but tragic day of landing, the First King's Own Scottish Borderers lost their Commander and more than half their men ; Jerusalem, Gaza and Damascus ; Macedonia and Doiran ; Megiddo and Bagdad ;

Archangel ; the Piave ; the Suez Canal. Scotland was there, at every one.

Then come names particularly associated in Scottish hearts with the four Scottish Divisions of the New Armies. Beaumont Hamel, that grim fortress-village which the Fifty-First Division captured on November 13th, 1916, thereby securing the high ground of the Somme Valley after four months, and bringing the British Army at last within sight of Bapaume and the road to Cambrai. Arras, where on Easter Sunday, 1917, Haig, in order to support Nivelle in his ambitious operations on the Aisne and the Chemin des Dames, launched an overwhelmingly effective attack upon the Vimy Ridge and up the valley of the Scarpe. No less than three of our four Scottish Divisions took part in that assault—the Ninth, Fifteenth, and Fifty-First. Indeed, thirty-eight Scottish battalions actually crossed the parapet ; for we must not forget that there were Scottish Regular battalions embedded in other Divisions of the New Armies, furnishing a leaven of tradition and experience to unseasoned fire and courage. Buzancy, where the Fifteenth

Division, serving with General Mangin's troops in the summer of 1918, quitted themselves so stoutly that the gallant Frenchmen erected a memorial upon the field of battle to commemorate the achievement of their ancient Allies —a rough stone pyramid, on each side of which you may see the thistle of Scotland encircled by the roses of France. It was erected upon the spot where the furthermost Scottish body was found—the body of a private of the Royal Scots Fusiliers. Lastly, the Hindenburg Line, where the Fifty-Second Division, transferred to the Western Front after three years of yeoman service elsewhere—they had been the last to evacuate Gallipoli and among the first to enter Jerusalem—stormed their way across the deep-set Canal du Nord with Haig's victorious troops in September, 1918, and did their share in the final triumphant clearing of the soil of France.

CHAPTER V

THE WINDOWS

NOW let us begin our inspection in detail. We will start with the windows. These should furnish a fitting prelude to our pilgrimage, for upon them is set forth, in practical detail, the whole history of the War as it affected the daily lives of the men and women of our country. Never was such a faithful record of actual facts presented in glass.

Take the first which meets our eyes in the south wall as we turn left after entering. It is one of four which depict the four seasons of the year, as the year was lived by us in those strange, far-off days.

The first represents Autumn, as the figure of a reaper, and the rowans and brambles, attest. In the centre panel is a depiction of that poignant moment, the arrival of the Leave Train. Note the completeness of detail in this brief space— the child on his father's shoulder, the newsboy, the coffee bar, the Jock with his captured helmet. Below are munition-makers at work—women. It was everybody's War.

The second, with its faggots, mistletoe, and holly, brings us to Winter. Last Post is being sounded in the snow. On the top of a cliff a motionless uniformed figure, silhouetted against the wintry sky, stands guarding the coast. A camouflaged convoy steals on its way : a hostile periscope peers out in vain.

Let us step east, to the other side of the entrance, and contemplate the other two windows of this series.

That on the extreme left, with its coltsfoot, primrose, anemone, and whin, conveys the promise of Spring. The ever-present perils of the home front are depicted—an air-raid, a blazing searchlight probing the dark skies, an anti-aircraft gun, an ambulance. We think again of that night in 1916, when Zeppelins rained destruction upon Edinburgh and the old Rock itself.

The last gives us Summer, with her wild roses, poppies, and thistles. A little boy, as yet untouched by man's warlike responsibilities, dives into a pool. Here is a departing troop-ship, another little masterpiece of detail, with her indispensable ally, the mine-sweeper; there, convalescent soldiers, in the well-remembered hospital blue. Or *is* it well-remembered? We may consider this later.

We turn next to the great window at the west end of the Hall, dedicated to the Air Services. We see aeroplanes, hydroplanes, airships, ob-servation balloons, even fluttering birds—all the emblems of Flight. The centre panels are united by an airship propeller. Below all is the badge of the Royal Air Force—the new arm which achieved such sudden eminence in those audacious years. How quickly we come to take things as a matter of course: in August 1914 such Army aeroplanes as we possessed were attached to something called the Balloon Sec-tion. Below the badge we note the sadly appro-priate epitaph: "*I bare you on eagle's wings, and brought you unto Myself*"—a truly faith-ful rendering of the Royal Air Force motto, *Per Ardua ad Astra.*

THE ROYAL NAVY WINDOW
(For description see p. 45)

To the left of the Air Force Window, in the south-west bay, is the Women's Window. It shows us two Land Girls, a Munition-Maker, a Red Cross Motor Cyclist, and Red Cross Nurses, steadfast in their several arduous tasks. Above, upon the keystone, we see the Pelican again, and a Lamp, to symbolize Sacrifice and Nursing.

At the other end of the Hall, facing the Air Force Window, is another of similar form and setting. This is dedicated to the Sea, and to all who go down thereto, as the dolphin, trident, and conch-shell of Neptune on the keystone imply. This window serves as more than a record of service : it is a Cenotaph in itself. Like the Menin Gate at Ypres, which commemorates the missing soldiers of the Salient, it serves as a headstone and epitaph for those who, to quote the words carved below, " *Have no other grave than the sea* ".

The activities of the Navy are depicted by four medallions—a destroyer travelling at full speed ; a troopship (the *Olympic*), zigzagging with the wise deliberation which we used to find so irksome ; the deck of a battleship, with the Forth Bridge in the distance—a reminiscence of the great (and now bygone) Base at Rosyth—and a submarine, submerged in the eerie, fishy depths. Below the window are carved the names of the principal naval battles of the War, and of British ships which acquired particular distinction in individual combat. So silent was our Navy about its achievements during those misty years, that some of the references here must be obscure to many, and a complete surprise to some. The epic duel, for instance, between the *Carmania* and the *Cap Trafalgar*, the only instance in the War of a direct naval encounter between two armed merchant cruisers—an encounter from which the gallant old Cunarder emerged with full honours—and the tale of how in the pitchy darkness of a stormy night off Dover, two British destroyers, *Swift* and *Broke*, engaged six German opponents and sank at least two of them.

Adjacent to this window, in the south-east bay, is another, depicting the Mechanism of War—Heavy Artillery, the Machine-Gun, the Tank, Bridge-building : in lesser prominence, a bomb-thrower, a flame-thrower, an armoured car, and a trench-cutting machine. How unfamiliar would most of this paraphernalia have appeared to a previous generation; and how much less familiar, *Deo volente*, will it appear to the generations yet to come.

CHAPTER VI

THE REGIMENTAL MEMORIALS

NOW we come to the monuments of stone and bronze, of which there is a most memorable array. First, the twelve Regimental Memorials, each comprising in effect a little shrine in itself, uniform in design, but with a wide margin for the arrangement of details of regimental history and tradition. These extend right round the Hall of Honour, and each is set between a pair of the columns which support the roof. Everywhere else, upon walls, piers, and lintels, are displayed the records of the other Services, great and small—from the noble bronzes of the Artillery and the Engineers to a tiny and rather moving little depiction, near the base of a pillar in the south-west bay, of a cage containing mice and canaries—" The Tunnellers' Friends ". The ruling idea has been that in this, a nation's Valhalla, no service, however slight or humble, shall be overlooked.

ONE OF THE TWELVE REGIMENTAL MEMORIALS : THE SCOTS GUARDS
(The closed book upon the lectern below the panel is the regimental Roll of Honour)

Let us now examine the Regimental Memorials. (You will note that you are being invited to make the circuit of the Hall thrice—once for the windows, once for the Regimental Memorials, and once for the rest. There is no other way : so rich are the treasures stored within these walls that whether your quest be for History, Beauty, or merely Remembrance, the attempt to absorb the whole in a single round must lead only to confusion and fatigue of mind.)

As already noted, these Memorials are more or less all of a pattern. Each consists of a shallow bay between two pillars. Upon the wall between the pillars is set a panel, surmounted by the Regimental Crest. Above come the coats-of-arms of two Scottish burghs or counties.[1] On each panel is a history of the regiment, told in a simple tale of names, dates, and battle honours. On either side hang the Colours.

But before we proceed with our examination, let us remember that whenever we speak of a

[1] These do not necessarily indicate the Regiment's territorial district.

D

regiment we are usually speaking of two regiments. Under the great scheme of reform instituted some sixty years ago by Lord Cardwell, the father of the present British Army, regiments which had existed hitherto as separate units, each with its own history and traditions, were frequently coupled together, under the " linked battalion " system, into what was practically a new regiment, with a common recruiting area and interchangeable personnel ; since when the history of every British regiment has been the joint history of its battalions But the pre-Cardwellian record of each is still, quite rightly, kept separate and distinct. You will find this fact emphasized more than once in the Memorials which we are about to examine : for instance, the old battle honours and badges of each battalion are frequently displayed in separate columns.

It should also be noted that when we speak of the date of the first raising of a regiment we are in point of fact referring, as a rule, to the raising of its First Battalion.

Below each panel stands a stone table, upon

THE LONDON SCOTTISH MEMORIAL

(Through the arch to the left, the King's Own Scottish Borderers Memorial)

which rests a leather-bound volume, containing the Regimental Roll of Honour. The lists within are by this time so thumbed and frayed by eager searchings as to be, in places, almost undecipherable. In due course, when every searcher has found the precious name, and anxious hearts are satisfied, a new and final Roll will be substituted.

II

We can take the Memorials in any order we please ; but perhaps it will be simplest to start in the south-west bay with the Camerons and the Argylls ; then work eastward along the north wall, where there are eight in a row, and finish in the south-east bay with the Gordons and the Scots Greys, ranged side by side here as they were at Waterloo.

THE SOUTH-WEST BAY

THE QUEEN'S OWN CAMERON HIGHLANDERS

In the lay mind there has always been a tendency, understandable enough, to confuse the Camerons with the Cameronians. But if we study the early history of these two famous regiments, no sort of excuse will remain for our ever confusing them again.

Never were two infants born in more widely different surroundings. The Cameronians, as we shall presently see, were of stout Lowland Covenanting stock, and were actually called into existence, at the time of the Revolution, to assist in making an end of King James II and the Stewart cause. The Camerons were of a very different breed. In the words of a contemporary chronicler, they were " a very potent Clan of Lochaber. The Laird of Lochiel is their Chief." Moreover they were Stewart loyalists to a man. Long before they gave their name to a regular regiment of the British Army they were busily engaged, as a clan, in causing that Army considerable trouble. They contributed largely to Dundee's victory at Killiecrankie, and it is highly probable that a few weeks later they actually encountered their almost-namesakes, the newly-embodied Cameronians, in the desperate struggle for

Dunkeld. They fought at Sheriffmuir in the 'Fifteen; they were out again in the 'Forty-Five, and suffered the penalties and forfeitures which followed on Culloden.

A generation later, in 1793, a surprising thing happened. Alan Cameron of Erracht, a kinsman of the Lochiel family, had fled to America to avoid the consequences of a duel. He fought as a Loyalist in the American War of Independence, and was taken prisoner. In due course he escaped, and returned to his native land. Here, with his new loyalty unshaken, he offered to raise a regiment from within the County of Inverness to serve King George III. Thus, burying the memory of past wrongs, the West Highlands came into line with their Lowland and English brethren.

The new regiment was composed essentially of Highland gentlemen, the officers themselves bearing the expense of raising it and accepting no bounties from the Government. Their present-day title was not conferred upon them at once: they were first called the Cameronian Volunteers; later, probably to avoid confusion

with the Cameronian Rifles, the Cameron
Highlanders.

The history of the Regiment soon became
part, and always an illustrious part, of the
history of the British Army. You have only
to peruse the list of battle honours to realize
that. *Egmont-op-Zee—Corunna—The Peninsula—
Waterloo—The Crimea—The Indian Mutiny—
Egypt—South Africa*—so runs the tale, vivid
enough in the barest outline. Their existence
as an individual unit was threatened more than
once—and not by the enemy. In the West
Indies, soon after their embodiment, they were
so reduced in numbers by privation and disease
that the survivors of the rank-and-file were
actually transferred *en masse* to the Forty-
Second, or Black Watch. But the officers, non-
commissioned officers and drummers returned
to Scotland, where they speedily found recruits
and resuscitated the old regiment. In 1881,
under the Cardwellian system of Army reor-
ganization, it was again suggested that they
should be linked with the Forty-Second, to
form the Second Battalion of the Black Watch.

But clan and regimental spirit rose high against the idea of submersion, and the suggestion was defeated—as was another, six years later, to convert the Cameron Highlanders into the Third Battalion of the Scots Guards. So for some time, this highly individual unit remained the only single-battalion regiment in the British Army.

Pride of Clan ruled throughout. Not a Cameron soldier could fall but every other Cameron felt it. In the Peninsula, on May 5th, 1811, at Fuentes d'Onor, where Massena made his desperate attempt to turn the British right flank and so relieve Almeida, Colonel Philips Cameron, son of the Alan Cameron who had formed the regiment, was shot by a sniper, and fell mortally wounded. The sequel can be imagined. There arose from the clansmen the grief-stricken cry " Thuit an Camshronach ! "— " Cameron has fallen ". Then, backed by the Connaught Rangers and the Highland Light Infantry, who understood Gaelic too, they fell upon the French Imperial Guard and swept them into oblivion. The man who had shot

Colonel Cameron fell pierced with countless wounds.   Sir Walter Scott has immortalized the scene :—

> . . . For Cameron slain,
> Wild from the plaided ranks the yell was given.
> Vengeance and grief gave mountain rage the rein,
> And, at the bloody spear-point headlong driven,
> Thy despot's giant guard fled like the rack of
> heaven.

The stone tablet before us breathes the same spirit of Highland pride. Upon most of the Regimental Memorials in this building a certain amount of space is devoted to details of the early history of the Regiment, a list of the battalions raised during the Great War, and the casualties suffered. Upon the Cameron Memorial these items are omitted—or perhaps taken for granted. In their place you will find an inscription in Gaelic. It is very similar both in tone and in wording to the English inscription set above it, but both seem necessary, for surely a part at least of the epitaph of men who " had the Gaelic " should be written in the sweet Gaelic tongue, however far from their native glens their graves may lie. The English inscription runs as follows :—

Remember with undying gratitude the loyalty and sacrifice of the Cameron Highlanders who laid down their lives during the Great War, 1914-1918.

Here is the Gaelic inscription :—

CUIMHNICHIBH · NA · SUINN.
NACH · MAIREANN
MAIRIDH · AN · CLIU BEO
GU · BRATH

Being interpreted, it means :—

Remember the heroes who are no more : their renown will live for ever.

Then follows a brief record of achievement in the Great War. To this may be added that the establishment of the Regiment was increased to eleven battalions, of which the Tenth consisted of Lovat's Scouts. To this gallant eleven we must add a twelfth—the Queen's Own Cameron Highlanders of Canada, whose Roll of Honour is lodged with that of the parent body within the Casket in the Shrine.

The Camerons fought in France, Belgium, and Macedonia.[1] Three hundred and sixty-five Officers and six thousand seven hundred and ninety Other Ranks in all gave their lives. In the Battle of Loos no less than five battalions of the Regiment participated — the First in the First Division, the First-Fourth in the Seventh, the Fifth in the Ninth, and the Sixth and Seventh in the Fifteenth. The Fifth, in their successful attack on the Hohenzollern Redoubt, were commanded by Cameron of Lochiel. Lieut.-Colonel A. F. Douglas-Hamilton, who commanded the Sixth, fell in circumstances of extraordinary gallantry while leading his men for the fourth time in an attack on Hill 70. He was awarded a posthumous V.C.

Such, in brief, are the history and traditions of this proud and distinguished regiment. Many brave men not of the Cameron name have won distinction in their ranks, particularly during the Great War ; but their pride was, and still is, mainly local and tribal. Lochiel out

[1] If we include the Lovat Scouts, they fought in Gallipoli, Sinai, and Salonika as well.

with his own, from Killiecrankie to Loos—that is the Cameron formula.

PRINCESS LOUISE'S
ARGYLL AND SUTHERLAND HIGHLANDERS

As a contrast to the Camerons, who existed during half their history as a single-battalion regiment, we now have the Memorial tablet of a corps which until the time arrived for automatic amalgamation under the Cardwellian system consisted of two entirely separate and distinct regiments—the Argyll Highlanders and the Sutherland Regiment—the Ninety-First and Ninety-Third.

The Argyll Regiment was raised in 1794 by Lieut.-Colonel Duncan Campbell of Lochnell, and as might be expected was at first a thorough-going Campbell unit, wearing the Campbell tartan and having more than half of its officers Campbells.

Shortly after their embodiment the Argyll Highlanders entered upon a period of service in the Peninsula which was to make their name historic. Their first great test was the Retreat to Corunna, perhaps the greatest rear-guard action in all our history. In the depths of winter, with an army of raw and inexperienced troops, lacking food, fuel, and even boots, hard pressed by two of Napoleon's ablest marshals, Soult and Ney, Sir John Moore battered his way to the sea, without the loss of a gun or the breaking of a line of his rear-guard. He died in the moment of victory; but he had lured Napoleon away from Lisbon and saved Portugal. Scotsmen may be proud to remember that among his tattered army of heroes were numbered no less than seven Scottish regiments, each of which now rightly wears the name *Corunna* on its Colours. The Argylls formed part of the rear-guard. They covered eighty miles and fought seven times in the space of twelve days.

They again distinguished themselves in the later stages of the Peninsular War, after the British Army had scaled the barrier of the Pyrenees and invaded the soil of France. Waterloo they missed, being sent to guard the road to Brussels; but it is consoling to note that the first individual of the Allied Forces to enter

Paris after the battle was a drummer of the Ninety-First, bearing the flag of truce.

Two other Argyll memories, of a totally different kind, are the stories of the *Birkenhead* and the *Abercrombie-Robinson*—both epics of the sea. The story of the *Birkenhead* is told more fully elsewhere in this volume.[1] A detachment of the Ninety-First were on board, and went down with the rest, unflinchingly, ungrudgingly, as the women and children drew off into safety.

The *Abercrombie-Robinson* went ashore in a raging storm in Table Bay, in August 1842. She had on board four hundred and fifty-six men of the Ninety-First, one hundred and nine women and children of their families, a detachment of the Cape Mounted Rifles, and some sick men. Surf-boats were procured from the shore, and within four hours every soul had been safely landed. The men of the Ninety-First declined to leave the ship until their women and children and all the other men were safe on the beach.

[1] See Highland Light Infantry.

The Ninety-Third was in a sense senior to the
Ninety-First, as it grew out of the Sutherland
Regiment, a corps which had been raised by
Wemyss of Wemyss (the heir-male of the
Duchess of Sutherland) as early as 1779.
General Wemyss's method of enlistment, it is
interesting to note, was to line up all the likely
young men in the district and offer them each a
pinch of snuff from his own mull. After such
a compliment from the Chieftain himself, re-
fusal of service was out of the question. However, it was not until 1799 that the Sutherland
Regiment was formally embodied ; so the
Argyll Regiment, when amalgamation came in
1881, took pride of place as First Battalion.

As the name of the Ninety-First is for ever
associated with the Peninsula, so is that of the
Ninety-Third with the Crimea and the Mutiny.
In the Crimean War they served in the illustrious
Highland Brigade, together with the Black
Watch and the Camerons. At Balaclava the
Regiment formed that historic " thin red streak,
tipped with a line of steel," which, only five
hundred and fifty strong and formed two-deep,

faced, withstood, and repelled an attack of twenty-five thousand Russians. " I did not think it worth while to form them four-deep ", said Sir Colin Campbell afterwards—and he was right.

But the most brilliant achievements of the Sutherland Regiment came in the Mutiny. They were with Sir Colin Campbell at the Relief of Lucknow—a seasoned regiment a thousand strong, of whom seven hundred wore the Crimea medal. In point of fact Sir Colin relieved Lucknow twice. On the first occasion he raised the siege of the Residency and contrived, in the very teeth of the enemy, to evacuate six hundred women and children, with some thousand sick and wounded men. This notable feat had barely been accomplished when he received the news that Nana Sahib was attacking Cawnpore, directly on his lines of communication. Taking his helpless convoy with him—many of them died by the way, but he dared not leave them—he hastened to Cawnpore, routed the enemy, then returned without pause to complete the relief of Lucknow, where

Outram was still holding on against overwhelming odds. In the tremendous battle which followed, and which ended in the entire recapture of the city, the Ninety-Third were entrusted with the assault upon the Begum's Palace, or Sikandarbagh, which was more solidly built and more desperately defended than any other stronghold. At length a small breach was created in the wall. Which of the Ninety-Third was the first to get through is still a matter of debate, but the Palace fell, and six Victoria Crosses were the result. And so in the single word *Lucknow*, emblazoned upon the Regimental Colours, are comprised not one battle but two, with a forced march and the battle at Cawnpore thrown in. In commemoration of this resounding achievement Sir Colin Campbell was appointed Colonel of the Ninety-Third.

In 1881 the two regiments were united, under the name of Princess Louise's Argyll and Sutherland Highlanders, in honour of the daughter of Queen Victoria, who had recently been married to the Marquis of Lorne, future Duke of Argyll.

Her Royal Highness is still Colonel-in-Chief of the Regiment.

By the end of the century both battalions were serving abroad. The Second came victoriously through the Tochi Valley campaign, while the First participated in the grim but useful lessons of the South African War.

In 1914, when the great call came, the First Battalion were hurried home from India, while the Second went to France with the Expeditionary Force. They were the first to cross the Channel and the last to retreat from Mons. The Regiment as a whole was expanded to twenty-seven battalions. For the tale of their combined sacrifice and achievement we have but to contemplate the Memorial before us. They fought in France, Belgium, Macedonia, Gallipoli, and Palestine. Four hundred and thirty-one Officers and six thousand four hundred and seventy-five Other Ranks gave their lives. Truly, the spirit of Corunna, Balaclava, and Lucknow is in no wise abated.

E

THE NORTH WALL

THE HIGHLAND LIGHT INFANTRY

(CITY OF GLASGOW REGIMENT)

Here is another Memorial, commemorating the service of two ancient and distinguished units, blended just fifty years ago into a famous modern regiment—a regiment which during the Great War expanded itself into twenty-six battalions. Fifteen of these served overseas, upon every front from Ypres to Mesopotamia and from Gallipoli to Archangel. Of those who served, just under ten thousand gave their lives —a record of devotion which seems to lie outside the bounds of clumsy human comment.

As for regimental history, the First Battalion of the Highland Light Infantry were originally the Seventy-Third, or Macleod's Highlanders. They were raised in 1777, that most prolific period in Scottish military history, by John, Lord Macleod, eldest son of the Earl of Cromarty, mainly from his own clan and the Mackenzies. John Macleod had been out in the 'Forty-Five—the *Bliadhna Thearlaich*, or Year of Charles—and the raising of the Seventy-Third Regiment was a wise move on his part, as it probably kept his head on his shoulders. The Seventy-Third, incidentally, were the first clan regiment ever raised for the King's service in Scotland: the Seaforths and the Camerons came just after.

Almost immediately upon their embodiment the Regiment were sent out to India, where they remained for close on eighteen years. Their first experience of battle was tragic. During a jungle march near Perambucam the two flank companies of the Regiment, under Captains David Baird and John Lindsay, while advancing with other troops to join Sir Hector Munro and the main army, were assailed by Hyder Ali in overwhelming force with fifty-seven cannon. The whole detachment was annihilated. The men of the Seventy-Third fought to the end in ever-diminishing squares, and actually repelled thirteen charges. When all was over, the handful of survivors, though quarter had been promised them, were chained together two and two, and thrown to rot in underground dungeons.

A year later Sir Eyre Coote, by a crushing defeat of Hyder Ali on almost exactly the same ground, did something to avenge this memory. To-day the episode is chiefly remembered by the grimly humorous observation of an old Scottish lady, mother of Captain David Baird, upon hearing her son's fate :—" Lord pity the man that 's chained to oor Davie ! "

Thereafter the Seventy-Third Regiment— soon to be renumbered, in 1786, the Seventy-First—was engaged in almost every campaign in which the British Army have fought. To-day the Highland Light Infantry can boast a longer Roll of Battle Honours than any regiment in the British Army, with the sole exception of the King's Royal Rifle Corps. They helped to garrison Gibraltar through a long siege. They fought in Moore's immortal retreat to Corunna. They fought right through the Peninsular War. They fought at Waterloo. They seem to have fought everywhere.

Meanwhile another regiment had come to birth which was destined in the fulness of time to become the " opposite number " and fight-

ing-mate of the Seventy-First. This was the
Seventy-Fourth, raised in 1787 by Major-
General Sir Archibald Campbell. The Regiment was, in its early days, closely identified
with the Campbell interests, and wore the dark-
green tartan of the Clan.

Like the Seventy-First, the Seventy-Fourth
went to India almost immediately. They so
greatly distinguished themselves at the Battle of
Assaye that they were called " The Assaye
Regiment " for a century after. You will see
their device, an elephant superscribed " Assaye "
—a distinction shared by the Seaforth Highlanders—carved upon the Memorial before us.
They acquired further merit during the Peninsular War, but arrived in Flanders just too late
for Waterloo.

One of their proudest achievements, of an
entirely different kind, is the immortal episode
of the *Birkenhead*, when six hundred and thirty-
one British soldiers, including Colonel Seton
and sixty-six men of the Seventy-Fourth, stood
resolutely to attention upon the deck of a sinking
troopship that room might be found in the boats

for their women and children, every one of whom was saved. Furthermore, when the ship went down, they refrained from swimming to the already crowded boats, for fear of endangering their occupants. Little wonder that the King of Prussia, afterwards first German Emperor, should have ordered the story of the *Birkenhead* to be posted up in every barrack-room of his Army.

It is upon such memories as the last that the mind is most prone to linger, within these walls. We realize, suddenly and sometimes tardily, that the soldier is after all something more than a fighting machine : he is a man, more readily moved by an appeal to his manhood than by any mechanical direction, however perfect. On three occasions in their recorded history, for instance, the Highland Light Infantry have been rallied and heartened by the skirl of the pipes. In the heat of the battle at Porto Novo in 1780, where eight thousand British troops found themselves pitted against Hyder Ali with a hundred thousand, Sir Eyre Coote, the Commander-in-Chief, had reason to note the electric effect upon the Seventy-First of their pipers' zeal and courage. As a memento, he afterwards presented to the Regiment a set of silver pipes. Again at Vimiera, a piper of the Glasgow Highland Regiment—as the Seventy-First were at that time called—one George Clark, though wounded and unable to share in the advance, cried :—" Deil hae me, lads, if you shall want for music ! " and struck up a tune as he lay. The " lads " heard him, and advanced to victory. In the assault on Badajoz another piper, Maclachlan, of the Seventy-Fourth this time, was first in the escalade, playing *The Campbells are Coming*. " He headed the advance along the rampart," we are told, " till his pipe-bag was pierced by shot ; then he sat down on a gun-carriage, and heedless of the bullets which flew about him, calmly repaired the damage and resumed his tune." Maclachlan died at Vittoria a few years later, piping to the end, with both legs shot off. No wonder the Scottish regiments are proud of their music—the finest battle music in the world. In 1810, when the Seventy-First were converted into a Light Infantry

Regiment, and their kilts were irrevocably replaced by trews, they fought, and fought successfully, to retain their pipers. They have them still.

But perhaps the picture of all others upon which the memory lingers is one of the Seventy-Fourth while on garrison duty in Madrid. Here they were so moved by the utter destitution of the wretched inhabitants, that out of their own scanty supplies they provided a daily dinner " for two hundred persons, who otherwise would have perished ". The thought of those rough, un-tutored, and possibly hungry Jocks, sharing their rations with a handful of starving women and children in a foreign city, will survive in many a heart long after the glories of Assaye and Waterloo and Ypres have faded into oblivion.

THE CAMERONIANS
SCOTTISH RIFLES

The old title, " The Cameronians ", you will observe, still survives. Efforts have occasionally been made by Whitehall to eliminate it, but it goes on—and rightly. That title is History— the History of Scotland and Presbyterianism.

The Cameronians took their name from Richard Cameron, the founder of the Reformed Presbyterian Church, who was executed for " treason " in 1680 ; but many of them were seasoned soldiers long before they were actually embodied as a regiment—fighting on the side of the Covenant in the illusory success of Drumclog in 1679, and later in the disaster of Bothwell Brig.

But on April 29th, 1689, the " Cameronian Whigs " sprang suddenly into existence as a complete fighting unit. James II had lost his throne, and his ever loyal supporter Claverhouse had hastened south to rouse the clans to what might be a successful effort to put him back there. Something, therefore, had to be done to save the Covenant, and done quickly. In one day then, at Douglas, " without beat of drum or the expense of levy money ", the Cameronian Regiment was raised and embodied, with the young Earl of Angus as its Colonel ; and four months later, by its desperate and successful

defence of Dunkeld, entirely reversed the situation created by Claverhouse's victory at Killiecrankie, and saved Scotland for Presbyterianism
—and for William and Mary.

A regiment founded in such an environment
and constructed of such material was bound to
have certain definite and unusual traditions of
its own. The organization of the Cameronian
Regiment was that of a Presbyterian congre-
gation. Every man carried a Bible ; each
company had to provide one Elder. The
memory of the years when they had worshipped
in hillside conventicles, with sentries out on the
horizon against the King's troops, was carefully
preserved. To this day, when the First
Battalion hold Church Parade in camp or the
open, they do so fully armed, Bible in belt.
Picquets are sent out and sentries posted ; and
not until the picquet reports " all clear " does
the Commanding Officer instruct the Minister
to proceed with the service. At Mess, too, the
King's health is honoured sitting, not standing.
Standing among the Covenanters was, and is,
the attitude of prayer ; therefore to stand in

honour of the King would be to render unto Caesar the things that are of God. So they sat, and sit.

Like all "powerfully prayerful" regiments, the Cameronians have always been "bonny fechters", as their list of battle honours indicates. Almost immediately after their embodiment they were engaged in Marlborough's four historic battles—Blenheim, Ramillies, Oudenarde, and Malplaquet. They were with Moore at Corunna : they helped to win North America and the West Indies from the French. They helped to drive Napoleon from Egypt, and they wear the Sphinx to prove it. The other badge here displayed, the Dragon, commemorates their service in the China War of 1840. Later, they went through the twin horrors of the Crimea and the Indian Mutiny. The above, of course is a tale of joint achievement. Sometimes it was one battalion, sometimes the other. It is well to remember that for nearly a century the Second Battalion fought under another name, that of the Perthshire Light Infantry, or 90th Foot. Their romantic origin must be briefly described here : it differs strangely from that of their " opposite number ".

In 1789 a Scottish Laird, Thomas Graham of Balgowan, was returning home from the South of France, carrying with him the dead body of his young wife for burial in Scotland. At Toulouse the Revolutionary mob, then at the height of its excesses, laid violent hands upon the sad little cavalcade, opened the coffin, and offered other insults both to living and dead. Thereafter Graham lived only for revenge. When he reached home he raised a regiment to fight the French. They were called the Perth-shire Volunteers—later, the Perthshire Light Infantry—and are now the Second Battalion of the Scottish Rifles. It was they who fought in Egypt, the West Indies, the Crimea and through the Mutiny.

As for the joint record of the twenty-seven Cameronian battalions in the Great War, is it not written on the tablet before us ? *To the Glory of God*, it runs—*and in memory of 7075 Officers, Warrant Officers, Non-Commissioned Officers, and Men who served in the Regular,*

Special Reserve, Territorial, and Service Battalions in the Great War, 1914-1918, and laid down their lives for King and Country, this monument is placed in the capital city of their land, that what they did may not be forgotten by their countrymen.

France, Belgium, Gallipoli, Egypt, Macedonia, Palestine—that is where they lie to-day. Richard Cameron and Thomas Graham must be proud of them.

THE ROYAL SCOTS FUSILIERS

The Royal Scots Fusiliers were raised in 1678, after the Restoration. Cromwell had taught Britain the meaning of a modern army, and Charles II was determined to have one of his own, in order to police his newly-regained kingdom—or, in Scotland, to keep the Covenanters in due submission. Accordingly Charles, fifth Earl of Mar, was commissioned to raise a regiment for the purpose, from the districts along the Highland line—Aberdeen, Angus, Stirling, and Renfrew—and thus the

Royal Scots Fusiliers came to birth. They
were familiarly christened " The Earl of Mar's
Greybreeks ", and were immediately sent to
hold down the Covenanting south-west. By
the irony of Fate the Covenanting south-west
became their ultimate recruiting-ground. The
Regimental Depot is now at Ayr.

They took no particular part in the events of
the Revolution, and in due course found themselves in the (at first) not altogether congenial
service of William III, who sent them out to
Flanders. Here they achieved distinction at
once, during those campaigns in which William's
chief task and difficulty lay in imposing some
kind of unity upon an ill-assorted alliance of
Dutchmen, Spaniards, Germans, and British
against the glittering power and might of
Louis XIV.

At this time nearly half the British Army in
Flanders consisted of Scottish troops. The
Royal Scots were there ; so were the King's
Own Scottish Borderers and the Cameronians.
They were not of course called by these names,
neither were they numbered. As often as not a

regiment was known by the name of its commander—a dizzy business for future historians.
Thus, the Royal Scots were the Douglas Regiment; the Cameronians, Munro's; and the
King's Own Scottish Borders, Leven's Regiment. The Royal Scots Fusiliers were
O'Farrell's Regiment. In 1694, however, the
numerical system was introduced. But instead
of being arranged in order of seniority, the
regiments were numbered according to the
date of their actual assignment to the English
establishment—in other words, of their first
arrival in England. This fell hardly on the
Scots and Irish regiments. The Royal Scots
Fusiliers, who should have ranked as Fourth
Regiment of the Line (senior indeed to the
famous Seventh Royal Fusiliers of London)
were allotted the numeral Twenty-one. They
accepted the situation, and proceeded to render
that numeral illustrious through the next two
centuries.

We are not concerned here to follow them in
their subsequent adventures, except in brief.
They fought in Marlborough's great campaigns:

Blenheim, *Oudenarde*, *Ramillies*, *Malplaquet* are inscribed upon their Colours. About this time they were created a Royal Regiment, and were named the Royal North British Fusiliers—a title which they retained until 1877.

They greatly distinguished themselves at Dettingen, under one of their most famous commanders and an outstanding character of his time, Sir Andrew Agnew of Lochnaw. It was he who, by way of indicating to his men their immediate objective in this battle, issued the pithy and historic Operation Order :—" My lads, ye see thae loons on yon hill there ? If ye dinna kill them, they 'll kill you ! " His men took the hill.

Perhaps their finest achievement was at Inkerman, where by their defence of The Barrier and their assistance in the capture of Shell Hill they were adjudged to have contributed more than any others to the victorious issue of the day. One of every three officers and men was killed or wounded : on Shell Hill itself the furthest limit of the British advance was marked by the bodies of three men of Number One Company of the dogged "Fusilier Jocks". Inkerman Day is still celebrated in the First Battalion by the trooping of the Colours.

As for their record in the Great War, we have but to lift our eyes and read. There were eighteen battalions, and they fought in France, Belgium, Gallipoli, Macedonia, Egypt, and Palestine. Three hundred and nineteen Officers gave their lives, and five thousand six hundred and forty-four Other Ranks. Perhaps the outstanding achievement of the Regiment during these years was the defence by the Second Battalion, for ten whole days against overwhelming odds, of a key position in the First Battle of Ypres, but for which the whole line must have crumbled and the enemy have broken through, perhaps to the Channel ports.

The most noticeable feature of this Memorial —perhaps the most beautiful Regimental Memorial in the building—is a space in the centre, surrounded by a carved wreath of laurel, devoted to a passage from Pericles' historic oration, quoted by Thucydides, upon the

F

Athenians who perished in the Peloponnesian War :—

The whole earth is the tomb of heroic men, and their story is not graven in stone over their clay, but abides everywhere without visible symbol, woven into the stuff of other men's lives.

A noble epitaph, and a great parallel. Three continents are the tomb of the Hundred Thousand Dead commemorated in this place. May the memory of their achievement remain for ever woven into the stuff of our own lives.

THE SCOTS GUARDS

This Memorial presents a unique and interesting feature in the form of an encircling frame of Company badges, interwoven with battle honours. Company badges are a distinctive Guards decoration, and the Scots Guards boast twenty-four of them. They were originally the devices borne on the Colours at the time when each company had its own Colours. The first were granted by King Charles II in 1650, and as additional companies

THE 'SUMMER' WINDOW

(For description see pp. 43-44)

were raised new Colours were given. The devices were altered from time to time, the principal changes taking place in 1707, the date of the Union.

The Scots Guards came to birth in the clash of civil war—in which experience they are not alone in Scottish military history. They were embodied in 1642, under the Marquis of Argyll, to go over and help the Protestant settlers in Ulster, who were having a bad time of it. Scotland was to supply the men for this expedition, while the English Parliament found the money. The money from England was not always forthcoming, but the men from Scotland fulfilled their part of the bargain. It took them seven years, but they saved Ulster for the Crown.

Upon their return home the " Irish Companies ", as they were called, assumed their normal function as protectors of the person of King Charles II. They soon had to reckon with Cromwell and his Ironsides, however. They suffered heavily at Dunbar, and were all but annihilated at Worcester. They were reconstituted at the time of the Restoration, under the name of the Scottish Foot Guards, and helped to defeat the Covenanters—forebears of the present Cameronian Regiment—at Bothwell Brig. Since then their history has been continuous. They have had various names—in 1713 they became the Third Guards and in 1831 the Scots Fusilier Guards—but in 1877 Queen Victoria gave them back their original title, the Scots Guards, which they have retained ever since.

In 1686 the Regiment was brought on to the English Establishment. One battalion abandoned Scotland to join the rest of the Brigade of Guards in London, the other battalion following in 1713. So closely did they become identified with the Brigade of Guards as a whole that Scotland never saw them again for two hundred years. It was 1911 before they returned, when they formed the Guard of Honour attendant upon King George V during his state visit to Edinburgh and Glasgow at the outset of his reign.

As for the purely military history of the Regiment, it will suffice to say that they speedily established those standards of efficiency and traditions of conduct which distinguish the Guards to-day—perfect discipline, scrupulous punctilio in the performance of routine duties, and a certain stately formality even in the rough-and-tumble of battle. There is a famous story of how, in 1745, at Fontenoy, as the Brigade of Guards stood deployed for action against the serried ranks of the French Guard, only fifty yards away, Lord Charles Hay of the First Guards stepped forward with a flourish of his plumed hat and ceremoniously consulted his French opponent as to which side should open fire first. We do not fight quite like that nowadays, but coolness in the face of the enemy is still the cardinal virtue of the soldier ; and those of us who saw the Guards go into action at a critical moment in the Battle of Loos, as unhurried and unruffled as for a ceremonial parade at Chelsea or Caterham, must have realized that the spirit of Fontenoy still lived after nearly two centuries.

The history of the Scots Guards is of course closely bound up with the history of the Brigade of Guards. *Tria Juncta in Uno*. They fought through the Peninsular War, to the finish and after—for they were still lustily attacking Bayonne in April 1814, ignorant that Peace had been signed. They fought at Waterloo as a unit of the Guards Brigade which held on to Hougomont all during that long and desperate Sunday afternoon until they had cleared the courtyard for the last time, slammed the great gate, and established their position once and for all. " The success of Waterloo ", wrote the great Duke long after, " turned upon the closing of the gate of Hougomont ".

They fought through the Crimea, and like everybody else concerned suffered terribly, chiefly from cold, sickness, and the gross mismanagement of the campaign. (Do you remember Lady Butler's famous picture of the Grenadier Guards paraded for Roll Call after Inkerman ?) They fought in Egypt at Tel-el-Kebir and Abu-Klea. This was not their first experience of Egypt, for they already wore the badge of the Sphinx, won by service in Sir Ralph Abercromby's victorious campaign of 1801.

They fought through the South African War, a campaign fruitful in " regrettable incidents " and broken reputations ; but during the whole of that long and sometimes demoralizing experience " no Scots Guardsman surrendered himself as a prisoner of war, and not a man was unaccounted for on parade when the rolls were called ".

For their record in the Great War you have but to contemplate the Memorial before your eyes. They were early in France, with the First and with the Seventh Division, and thereafter were to be found wherever the Guards were needed most. The casualties of their two battalions numbered two thousand eight hundred and forty-one. And everywhere—in mud, blood, and squalor—the stately pride of Fontenoy and the unbreakable front of Waterloo went with them.

THE ROYAL SCOTS

(THE ROYAL REGIMENT)

This, our most ancient Scottish regiment—subsequently known, when precedence was settled and numbers allotted, as the First Foot—

was raised as long ago as 1633, under the command of Sir John Hepburn. It was embodied by order of King Charles I and lent to King Louis XIII for service in France. But its history, authentic if unofficial, goes back much further than that—two centuries at least ; for it has its roots in the days when Scotland was the ally of France against the ancient enemy, England, and the person of the French monarch was protected by a Scottish bodyguard—as we may read in the pages of *Quentin Durward*.

Speedily this newly - created regiment attracted and absorbed into itself the majority of that scattered host of landless, expatriated Scots who were serving as mercenaries in the endless series of European wars—in the Netherlands, in Bohemia, in Denmark. A notable contingent was furnished by the remnants of the so-called Green Brigade, who had fought under Gustavus Adolphus, the Lion of the North. Two years after its foundation Le Regiment d'Hebron (the French rendering of Hepburn) numbered over eight thousand of all ranks.

In due course the Douglas Regiment—so called, according to the custom of the time, after the name of their current commander, but shortly to be re-christened the Royal Regiment of Foot—came back to the land of their birth, and took regular rank in the Royal Army of England—from 1633, the date of their embodiment. Thereafter they were constantly employed : you have only to scan their record of service to realize that. The names of Tangier, Sedgemoor (the last battle fought on English soil), Steenkirk, Blenheim, Fontenoy, Culloden, Louisburg, Havannah, Corunna, Egypt, the Peninsula, Niagara, Waterloo, India, Burma, the Crimea, China, and South Africa are an index of their activities. At one time they had four battalions on active service. In 1814 the Royal Scots, as they had now become, were fighting simultaneously in America, India, the Peninsula, and Holland. Their list of battle honours is a *précis* of Imperial history, and has been for nearly three centuries.

Mention of America reminds us that the Royal Scots greatly distinguished themselves in the Anglo-American War of 1812-1814. That campaign is little remembered in this country, for at that time we were at death-grips with Napoleon—the only country left standing up against him. It arose out of a dispute over the Right of Search—a right which the British Navy of those days exercised somewhat freely in its everlasting quest for recruits for His Majesty's service, many of whom were undoubtedly serving, for prudent reasons, under neutral flags—particularly the American flag. It was an intense and bitter war, and after three years ended with the dispute still undecided. The Americans actually burned Toronto; the British retaliated by capturing Washington and burning the White House. The Royal Scots won fame and the right to the battle honour *Niagara*, in fierce fighting along the Canadian border. They were not present at the Battle of New Orleans, the one serious reverse of the campaign, where a fine British force, largely composed of Peninsula veterans, were launched against an impregnable position, and heavily repulsed. By the irony of Fate this battle, the last ever fought, or ever likely to be fought, between British and Americans, occurred after Peace had already been signed.

Such a regiment has naturally fathered many famous men—some of them now almost legendary figures. There was Sir Robert Douglas, who commanded the Royal Scots at Steenkirk in 1692, and who, when a Colour of the Regiment had been captured by the enemy, leaped over a hedge, seized it from the French officer who was holding it, and threw it back to his men. But he did not come back himself: he fell gloriously, pierced with many wounds. And there was the Earl of Dumbarton, Commander of the Regiment in 1688. He could not reconcile himself to the *régime* of Dutch William, so went into voluntary exile with James II, sacrificing the career of a soldier rather than desert the cause for which he had fought all his life.

As for the record of the Royal Scots in the Great War, how can the tale be told, or a tenth part thereof, within present limits, of a regiment which raised thirty-five battalions, which fought in France, Belgium, Gallipoli, Macedonia and Palestine, and of which five hundred and eighty-three Officers and ten thousand six hundred Other Ranks gave their lives ? Instead of attempting the impossible, let us listen to Lord Rosebery :—

" The Royal Scots have stamped their name on almost every battlefield in which our army has been engaged. They have been commanded and trusted by such consummate commanders as Turenne, Marlborough, and Wellington. It has indeed been their habit to fight all over the world : there is scarcely a region where they have not left their mark. That is the way with all our regiments, but the Royal Scots have been longer at it."

These words were written in 1915, when the reputation of the Royal Scots rested solely upon the achievements of its Regular battalions. The record of the Territorial and Service units of the Regiment who fought through the War has not affected their truth. It has enhanced it.

THE ROYAL ARTILLERY MEMORIAL.

(See p. 124)

THE KING'S OWN SCOTTISH BORDERERS

Of all the Scots regiments the King's Own Scottish Borderers seem most peculiarly entitled to set up their Memorial here on the Rock; for they were originally called the Edinburgh Regiment, and their badge is that of the Castle itself. "The Castle of Edinburgh," says the official description, "with the motto, *Nisi Dominus Frustra*."

That title recalls a stirring and critical period in our history. In the year 1688 William of Orange landed at Torbay, and in a few weeks was King of England. The Revolution had come at last: what was Scotland going to do? There was little doubt about the answer to that question, for Scotland had had quite enough of the Stewarts. But the decision had to be put into formal and legal shape. Accordingly a "Convention of Estates" was summoned; James II was declared to have forfeited the Crown, and William and Mary were formally accepted as King and Queen of Scotland.

But James Graham of Claverhouse—" Bonny

Dundee "—had a word to say to that. He had lived a King's man, and a King's man he would remain, until " low lay the bonnet of Bonny Dundee ". So in a famous and picturesque episode he stalked out of the Convention, metaphorically snapping his fingers at the grim old Covenanters whom he had harried so long and so ruthlessly, and, leaving the defence of the Castle itself to that stout soldier the Duke of Gordon, rode off to the Highlands, there to rally the Clans in a last desperate effort to restore the fortunes of King James II. *Victrix causa deis placuit, sed victa Catoni.*

Knowing full well what they might expect if he succeeded, the Covenanters promptly raised troops on their own account, and the Edinburgh Regiment was among the firstfruits of their energy.[1] Within four hours it was a thousand strong, and within four months it had fought its first battle, Killiecrankie. From that disastrous encounter with Highland broadswords little credit and less glory could be derived ; but so gallantly

[1] The Cameronian Regiment was raised about a month later, to meet the same emergency. *Q.v.*

THE YEOMANRY MEMORIAL
(See p. 126)

did the young Edinburgh Regiment, under their veteran commander the Earl of Leven, acquit themselves, that the grateful citizens of Edinburgh conferred upon them two striking distinctions. The first was the right to march through the streets of the city, at any time, with bayonets fixed and Colours flying; the second, the privilege of recruiting in the City "by beat of drum on any day of the week except Sunday, without first asking the permission of the Lord Provost". Both these customs are still punctiliously observed as occasion arises.

Thereafter the Borderers settled down as a regular unit of the Royal Army, and proceeded to make history. They fought in King William's Flanders campaigns, already mentioned, at the end of the seventeenth century; they twice helped to defend Gibraltar during a long siege; they suffered with the Scots Guards and the Black Watch at Fontenoy, and did particularly stout service at Minden. Towards the end of the eighteenth century they temporarily converted themselves into Marines, and participated in Howe's great victory, off Brest, in the Battle

of the First of June.   They helped to drive
Napoleon from Egypt, and to wrest various West
Indian colonies—those hapless pawns in the in-
ternational politics of the day—from their French
occupants.   Like all our troops in these tropical
campaigns, they suffered terribly from sickness.

Within more recent memory they have distinguished themselves in the Afghan War of 1878
(wherein Lord Roberts achieved fame and title
by his historic march to Kandahar) and in the
hard-fought Chitral and Tirah campaigns.
During the latter they were in action twenty-
three times.   They went, of course, through the
salutary experience of the South African War,
and formed part of the iron ring which finally
rounded up Cronje at Paardeberg.

In the Great War the establishment of the
Regiment was expanded to twelve battalions.
The First came home from India as a unit of the
Twenty-Ninth Division, to lose more than half
their strength on Y Beach in Gallipoli, in the
tragic but glorious landing of April 25th, 1915.
The Second served throughout with the Fifth
Division : by the end of the War both were

fighting on the Western Front. The newly-raised battalions were distributed among these four Scottish Divisions whose badges are displayed on the outer walls of the Memorial. The Sixth suffered particularly severely at Loos.

For honours the Regiment as a whole has practically all the great battles of the War to choose from : it was represented, sometimes two or three times over, at most of them. The Regimental Motto speaks truly : *Nec aspera terrent*. Its dead number three hundred and fifty-nine Officers and six thousand five hundred Other Ranks.

THE BLACK WATCH

ROYAL HIGHLANDERS

Our first speculation concerning the Black Watch must inevitably be as to how they got their name, and what it signifies.

Here is the story. In the period of smouldering unrest which elapsed between those two memorable upheavals, the 'Fifteen and the 'Forty-Five, when the Old Pretender had gone and the Young Pretender was yet to come, some unusually sensible person, realizing that most of the Highlanders were clansmen first and Jacobites after, took a practical step to win the confidence of this proud, little understood, Gaelic-speaking people.

" Come into King George's service," he said, " and help us to pacify your own country. In return we will restore to you the right to carry arms and wear the Highland dress. In other words, if you will join forces with us, we will undertake to treat you like the Highland gentlemen that you are."

This proposal worked like a charm, and in 1725 six " Independent " companies of Highlanders, raised from different clans, were embodied as a semi-military force, to keep vigil over the Highland border and supervise the enforcement of the Disarming Act. These "watchers" wore the somewhat sombre tartans of their commanders, Campbell, Lovat, Grant and Munro—a striking contrast to the bright scarlet of the King's Regulars—so they were called *Am Freiceadan Dubh*, or the Black Watch.

Highland gentlemen they certainly were, and

they meant the world to know it, as a famous story attests. Two privates of the newly-formed Black Watch were sent to London to gratify the curiosity of King George II, who had never seen a Highland soldier, and was anxious to examine their arms and equipment. Having been introduced by their commander into the Royal presence, they gave an exhibition of fighting both with the broadsword and that most effective weapon, the Lochaber axe. Upon their withdrawal, His Majesty presented each of them with a guinea—which gratuity the two Highland gentlemen duly passed on to the doorkeeper as they left the Palace.

In due course the Black Watch companies were expanded into a full-bodied regiment of the British Army, the Forty-Third—a number changed nine years later to the more familiar and famous Forty-Second. They adopted a new tartan, known henceforth as the Black Watch, or Forty-Second, tartan.[1] In 1745, under the

---

[1] Thus the Black Watch alone have a regimental tartan of their own. The other Highland regiments wear a clan tartan.

command of Sir Robert Munro of Foulis, they received their baptism of fire at Fontenoy, where they fought with the greatest courage, especially in the rear-guard action which covered the retirement of the disorganized Allied Forces before Marshal Saxe's victorious troops. One hundred and seventy-three years later—on November 11th, 1918, to be precise—a battalion of the Black Watch were crossing the field of Fontenoy once again, when by a trick of Fate they received upon this, their ancient battle ground, the news of the Armistice. But this time they were an advance-guard, not a rear-guard.

We next hear of them in America, in that momentous campaign which marked the end of French predominance in Canada and the Mississippi Valley. Here the Forty-Second played a distinguished part in the attack on Ticonderoga. Indeed, such favourable notice did they attract in exalted quarters that in 1758 they were endowed by King George II with the title of " The Royal Highland Regiment " ; and a Second Battalion was raised, which was destined to achieve much fame on its own account, not only under its original title but for nearly a century as a separate regiment altogether, the Seventy-Third.

In 1795 came a great episode in the history of the Forty-Second. The long war with France, which was to end only at Waterloo, was now in full operation. The British Army was fighting —not for the first nor the last time—in Flanders. On the 5th of January an otherwise unimportant skirmish took place for the possession of a Flemish village named Geldermalsen, in the course of which a British Light Dragoon regiment retreated before the French, abandoning two field-guns. This was too much for the Forty-Second, who, with Major Dalrymple at their head, charged the enemy, recovered the guns, and by their own efforts—the horses being disabled—dragged them back to safety. In acknowledgment of this gallant feat King George III conferred upon the Regiment the decoration of " a red vulture plume," which still proudly survives in the famous Red Hackle worn in the head-dress.

Thereafter, as duly recorded in other cases,

the history of the Black Watch is the history of
the campaigns of Britain. India (where the
newly-raised Second Battalion, with a certain
Ensign Arthur Wellesley, afterwards the great
Duke of Wellington, as one of its junior officers,
made its mark against Tippoo Sahib during the
Siege of Mangalore), Egypt, the Peninsula,
Waterloo (both battalions), the Crimea, the
Mutiny (during which the Forty-Second won
eight Victoria Crosses), Ashanti, Egypt again,
and South Africa—the tale of these cannot be
set down here ; but enough has been told to
indicate the history and spirit of the oldest
Highland regiment in the British Army. A
detachment of the Black Watch also participated in the heroic incident of the *Birkenhead*,
described elsewhere.[1]

The two battalions were finally reunited in
1881, under the old title of the Black Watch
(Royal Highlanders).

The tablet before us bears final witness to the
record of the Regiment during the Great War.
Twenty-five battalions there were in all, to

[1] See Highland Light Infantry.

which must be added three Canadian battalions. The Canadian Black Watch enjoy a high and justly deserved reputation in their native land, and their affiliation to the parent body across the water is a matter of proud gratification to both.

As for the battle honours of those four years, you have but to contemplate the list before you— it covers France, Belgium, Macedonia, Egypt, Palestine, Mesopotamia—in order to realize that the Red Hackle was as present and prominent as ever, whenever the Flag waved or the voice of Duty called. You will find the names of five hundred and sixty-six Officers and nine thousand four hundred and fifty Other Ranks inscribed in the Regimental Roll of Honour at the foot of the Memorial.

THE SEAFORTH HIGHLANDERS

ROSS-SHIRE BUFFS

We find ourselves before another Highland Memorial. Above it is set a great stag's head, with the motto *Cuidich'n Righ*—" Save the King ! "—and thereby hangs a tale, a tale which reaches back for seven centuries—of how King

Alexander III of Scotland, hunting in the Forest of Mar, was beset by a wounded and infuriated stag, and was in danger of his life when Colin Fitzgerald, chief of the Mackenzie Clan, crying " *Cuidich'n Righ!* ", dashed forward and killed the stag with his spear. In gratitude for his deliverance the King bestowed upon the young chieftain a stag's head as his armorial bearings, with his loyal ejaculation for a motto. Small wonder, then, that the Seaforth Highlanders, who wear the Mackenzie tartan and were founded by Kenneth Mackenzie, Earl of Seaforth, should display this proud emblem as their own.

In addition, the Regimental slogan and private pipe-tune, *Cabar Feidh* (The Horns of the Deer) derive their origin from the same episode.

The Regiment itself was embodied during the period, after the 'Forty-Five, of gradual acquiescence by the Highlands in the Hanoverian *régime*. In 1778 the Earl of Seaforth, in gratitude for the restoration, after forfeiture, of his ancestral estates, offered to raise a regiment to serve King George III. The offer was accepted, and the Seaforth Highlanders sprang into being.

As usual, we have to remember that we are dealing with the history of two separate units, for a Second Battalion, the Ross-shire Buffs, was raised under similar auspices in 1793. Prior to their amalgamation in 1881 the two battalions fought as the Seventy-Second and Seventy-Eighth Regiment respectively, winning their laurels as a rule in different fields.

A glance at the combined battle honours here displayed makes it plain that to recount the whole story of the Seaforth Highlanders it would be necessary to describe most of the campaigns of the British Army. *Carnatic*, *Cape of Good Hope*, *Java*, *South Africa*, *Sevastopol*, *Lucknow*, *Afghanistan*, *Egypt*, *Chitral*, *Paardeberg*—these are a bare *précis* of the Regiment's history during what we are accustomed, rather quaintly, to call the pre-War era.

But if any part of the Seaforth record is to be picked out for special mention it must be the achievements of the Regiment in India—pooling, as usual, the exploits of both battalions.

The Seventy-Second were in India from 1781 to 1797, during a critical period in the history of

John Company.   For fifteen years they took part
in the desperate struggle to break the power of
Tippoo Sahib.   They were prominent in the
capture of Seringapatam and Bangalore, and
found time in addition to cross to Ceylon and
help to secure that island from the Dutch, who
were the allies of the French, for the young
British Empire.

They were succeeded in India by the Seventy-
Eighth, who participated in the brilliant victory
of Assaye, where Wellesley defeated a Mahratta
host six times as great as his own.   For their
gallantry on this occasion they received the right
to bear on their colours and appointments " an
elephant, superscribed Assaye ".   You will see
the badge on the upper part of the Memorial,
above the Stag's head.

But the Seaforths' finest work in India was yet
to come.   In 1857 the Mutiny broke out, and
once again the Seventy-Eighth were at hand
when they were most wanted.   Having gazed
upon the horrors of Cawnpore, and sworn a deep
oath of vengeance, they marched with Havelock
to Lucknow, where the shot-torn Residency was

still holding out; and, as we know, assisted to prolong that historic resistance till Sir Colin Campbell arrived with more Highlanders and made the relief complete. Eight Victoria Crosses were awarded to the Regiment in that campaign. None could grudge them their proud title of " The Saviours of India ".

Another twenty years, and it was the turn of the Seventy-Second again. They marched with Roberts to Kandahar, covering three hundred and twenty miles in twenty-two days, and in company with the Gurkhas, who have always been the firm friends of the Highlanders, greatly distinguished themselves in the relief of the city.

In 1809 they had suffered the indignity of having the kilt taken from them and replaced by trews. Perhaps in recognition of their service in Afghanistan, this wrong was righted on their return home in 1882, after their formal amalgamation with the Seventy-Eighth. Since then both battalions have worn exactly the same uniform.

As for the Seaforth record in the Great War, the tale is here told, briefly but poignantly, in letters of enduring stone. Ten battalions were

raised.   On the Western Front, in Palestine, in
Mesopotamia they fought, and eight thousand
four hundred and thirty-two lives were given—
the lives for the most part of sturdy lads from the
glens of Ross and Cromarty and the Island of
Lewis.   But not entirely.   One battalion—the
Seventy-Second Highlanders of Canada—came
all the way from Vancouver.   They fought as
a unit of the famous Canadian Corps, from
August 1916 until the moment of victory.
Cuidich'n Righ !

THE SOUTH-EAST BAY
THE GORDON HIGHLANDERS

Famous and romantic is the story of the raising of the Gordon Highlanders.   In 1793 the
young French Republic declared war against
Great Britain, and it became immediately
necessary to increase the size of the British
Army.   The authorities had by this time
realized the value of the new recruiting ground
created by the establishment of better relations
along the Highland line, now that Jacobitism
was a thing of the past.   Accordingly it was

decided to raise another Highland regiment, to supplement those two fine young units, the Black Watch and the Seaforth Highlanders, which had been embodied in 1740 and 1778 respectively.

To raise a third harvest from ground which had already been reaped twice was not too easy ; but a public-spirited and patriotic chieftain, the fourth Duke of Gordon, undertook the task, with triumphant success. He was assisted, as all the world knows, by his beautiful Duchess, who rode round to the country fairs in Highland bonnet and Regimental jacket, rewarding each recruit with a kiss—an unofficial initiation into the King's service which appears to have been even more highly valued than the guinea which accompanied it as bounty money. Indeed, one young blacksmith, we are told, who had already withstood the blandishments of all the recruiting officers of the Guard and the Line, having yielded to her Grace, took the kiss and threw the guinea to the crowd.

The Regiment were actually embodied in June 1794, with the Duke's eldest son, the

Marquis of Huntly, as Commander. They were almost immediately sent out to garrison Gibraltar. At this time they were known as the Hundredth Regiment, but in 1798 the name was changed to the more familiar Ninety-Second—" under which number," says a contemporary historian, " they have often distinguished themselves, and on the twenty-six occasions upon which they met the enemy, from 1799 to 1815, the latter invariably gave way before them."

You will note that one of their badges is *The Sphinx, superscribed Egypt*—a distinction which they share with the other British regiments who helped to shatter Napoleon's dream of an Eastern Empire. Another distinction, shared only with the Ninetieth (Scottish Rifles), is the name *Mandora* upon the Colours. The battles of Mandora and Alexandria were fought within a few days of one another, in March 1801. The former consisted in a successful British advance from Aboukir Bay, which brought Sir Ralph Abercromby and his men within sight of Alexandria. Both the Ninety-Second and

THE REGIMENTAL MEMORIALS 111

Ninetieth were singled out for mention in Sir Colin's despatch next day. The Ninety-Second earned further distinction at the Battle of Alexandria, when the French took the offensive and were defeated. Owing to weakness in cavalry and artillery the British were unable to follow up their success. Still the Battle of Alexandria, though tactically unimportant, had far-reaching effects. It showed Napoleon that the British Army as well as the British Navy was a power to be reckoned with ; and it delivered Egypt from French occupation. The heaviest blow at Alexandria was the death of that beloved Scottish soldier Sir Ralph Abercromby, who, when mortally wounded, was carried from the field by a bodyguard of the Ninety-Second. His brother it was who raised the Seventy-Fifth Regiment, now the First Battalion of the Gordons.

Then came the Peninsula. In the immortal episode of Corunna they were one of Sir John Moore's seven Scottish regiments ; and they were to the fore again in the great campaign which drove the last remaining French troops from Spanish soil. One of their most notable achievements was the capture of Arroyo del Molinos, which, though strategically an unimportant affair, evoked a letter from the Duke of Wellington to say that, had not the record of the Regiment been so magnificent already, he would have considered it worthy to be inscribed on the Colours.   At Waterloo, in company with the Royal Scots Greys, the Gordons made history.   They formed part of the Ninth Brigade in the Fifth (Picton's) Division.   They went into action saddened by the death of their commander, that rare spirit John Cameron of Fassifern, who had been killed at Quatre Bras. In spite of this—or perhaps because of it—they fought with a fury which has rendered the occasion for ever memorable.   We have but to contemplate Lady Butler's glorious battle picture, " Scotland for Ever ! " to recapture the scene—the Greys thundering to the charge, the charge which totally destroyed a column of Napoleon's best troops and lost him two thousand prisoners and two Eagles, with the pipes skirling and the yelling Gordons racing beside them, clinging to their stirrup-leathers.

The tradition of regimental friendship between Greys and Gordons, founded then, has remained ever since. In 1865, when, after the Crimea and the Mutiny, British troops found themselves once more at home, the Greys and the Ninety-Second foregathered at Aldershot, and fêted one another. The Officers' Mess of the Second Battalion of the Gordon Highlanders still cherish a snuff-box made from the hoof of the last surviving charger of Balaclava, presented upon this occasion.

For the rest, the Regimental list of battle honours must tell the tale—the tale of constant service and constant distinction—from Corunna to Lucknow, from Lucknow to Tel-el-Kebir, from Tel-el-Kebir to Dargai, from Dargai to Ladysmith and Doornkop, and from there to the endless fronts of France, Belgium, and Italy, during the four years of Armageddon. In that fiery trial the Regiment increased to twenty-one battalions. Four hundred and fifty-three Officers and eight thousand six hundred and nine Other Ranks gave their lives.

At the head of this panel you will observe the

H

Regimental Crest—a stag's head, surmounting the single word *Bydand*—the motto of the Gordon clan. The origin and exact significance of the word is uncertain, but it is probably a form of the old Lowland Scots verb " to byde ", or " bide ". (The Gordon family originally came from Northumberland.) In that case it means " Standing Fast ". No motto could have been more appropriately bestowed or worthily upheld.

THE ROYAL SCOTS GREYS

Last of all comes the Memorial of Scotland's only cavalry regiment, and the oldest cavalry regiment in the British Army, originally raised during the troublous period of religious strife which followed the Restoration of Charles II. The Royal Scots Greys were embodied in the same year as the Royal Scots—1678. They were called the Greys from their grey uniforms, and not from their horses. The grey horses which have been a special feature of the Regiment were introduced in 1702.

After a period of uncongenial police work

A GLIMPSE OF THE SOUTH EAST BAY

(Note Haig Medallion at foot of pier, and Gordon Highlanders and Royal Scots Greys Memorials to the left, through the arches)

under " Bonny Dundee," chiefly occupied in harrying the Covenanters, the new Regiment left Scotland and crossed the sea to Flanders, for the first but not by any means the last time in their experience. From this moment their history is the history of almost every British campaign in which cavalry were employed. They helped to sweep the enemy from the field at Marlborough's four great victories—Blenheim, Ramillies, Oudenarde and Malplaquet. They increased their fame at Dettingen and Warburg. But their day of days was Waterloo, where they won their distinctive silver badge of the French Eagle. Their charge with the Union Brigade of Heavy Cavalry against the Emperor's finest troops, with the Gordons [1] racing beside them, is historic. " Those terrible grey horses—how they fight ! " said Napoleon.

And so the brave tale goes on. They took part in the charge of the Heavy Brigade at Balaclava, and participated in the brilliant cavalry dash under Sir John French which relieved Kimberley in the South African War.

[1] See the Gordon Highlanders.

In the Great War they found themselves fighting in a new, strange and, for a cavalryman, a tragic world.   The ruthless hand of science had revolutionized the conditions and traditions of warfare.   For four long years, except for a few months of brilliant work in the open from Mons to Ypres in 1914, and again just before the Armistice in 1918, the Royal Scots Greys and other mounted troops found themselves practically immobilized.   The duties of cavalry are —first and foremost to obtain information as to the movements of the enemy ; secondly, by interposing themselves as a mobile screen, to conceal from the enemy the disposition of their own troops ; thirdly, to engage the enemy's cavalry in action ; and fourthly, by timely shock tactics, to convert a retirement into a rout.   But in this new and strange era of aeroplane observation, wireless telegraphy, Tanks, and the state of perpetual siege warfare imposed by a line of trenches stretching from the North Sea to the Alps, the cavalry found their occupation gone. They could not reconnoitre, they could not screen, they could not charge.   Nevertheless

THE HAIG MEDALLION

(See p. 131)

they were there, eager and efficient, hoping against hope behind every great attack. More than once during the critical early days, when reinforcements were scarce, they dismounted, sent away their horses, and plied pick and shovel and bayonet with the best of them—even as their forebears had done at the capture of Schellenberg under Marlborough more than two hundred years before. In this service they had one hundred and fifty-four killed.

At last they found themselves back in the saddle. Their service in the Great War had begun stubbornly with the Retreat from Mons, in 1914; it ended triumphantly with the Pursuit into Mons, in 1918. The Royal Scots Greys trooper on the big bronze horse, who stands at the foot of the Rock in Princes Street Gardens to commemorate the previous service of the Regiment, may well be proud of the achievement and sacrifice of his successors, recorded up here on the summit of the Rock itself. Truly their reputation throughout their history has more than justified their proud motto " Second to None ".

CHAPTER VII

THE OTHER MEMORIALS

NOW let us make our third and final tour of the Hall of Honour. There is still much to see—a wealth of beauty and imagination in stone and bronze, in tablet and trophy.

Once more we begin at the doorway itself. And now at last we can give due attention to something which we cannot have failed to observe and admire upon our first entrance.

Directly over the doorway stands a radiant golden figure, set against a great circular panel of blue and gold and green—a background of Sun, Sea, Earth and Sky. The figure represents the Spirit of Man purified by the flames of Sacrifice. The flames still play about the feet : the left hand grasps a broken sword-blade, symbol of the End of War, while the right holds the hilt aloft—the Cross Triumphant. The eyes gaze into the Shrine ; indeed they seem to penetrate beyond, as if beholding a new

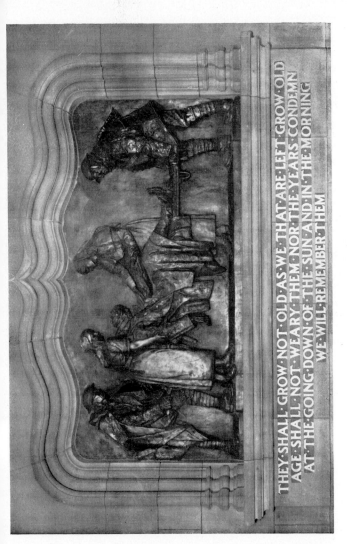

THEY·SHALL·GROW·NOT·OLD·AS·WE·THAT·ARE·LEFT·GROW·OLD
AGE·SHALL·NOT·WEARY·THEM·NOR·THE·YEARS·CONDEMN
AT·THE·GOING·DOWN·OF·THE·SUN·AND·IN·THE·MORNING
WE·WILL·REMEMBER·THEM

THE NURSING SERVICES PANEL.

(See p. 122)

Heaven and a new Earth.   The title of this noble composition is *Réveillé*.

On either side of the door are the two halves of the Royal Marine Memorial, with the badges of the Royal Marine Light Infantry and the Royal Marine Artillery, flanked by their appropriate colours.

Proceeding westward, and passing a trophy of ancient Scottish arms, set on a pillar between the Windows of Autumn and Winter—these trophies have their purpose, as we shall see—we come again to the south-west bay. The east, or inner wall, of this is largely occupied by the Memorial dedicated to a great brotherhood, nameless for the most part, whose dogged courage and unsleeping vigilance kept the high seas open for our commerce, and rendered our long and intricate coast-line immune from invasion for four years and more. Its members were the Mercantile Marine, the Royal Naval Reserve (including such notable units as the Tenth Cruiser Squadron which, strung across from Shetland to Iceland, held the gateway of the North Sea secure, week in week out, against contraband of War seeking entrance and enemy raiders seeking exit), the Royal Naval Volunteer Reserve, the Mine-sweepers (manned chiefly by stout-hearted East Coast fishermen), the Q ships, with their almost fabulous tale of adventure, and the Auxiliary Patrols—trawlers and drifters, with here and there a private yacht. By the end of the War some three thousand of these flimsy, plucky little vessels were patrolling home waters and protecting our coast.

In the upper part of the Memorial you will notice a circular bronze panel, depicting a merchant ship and a mine-sweeper at sea by night; below, this inscription :—

To the Officers and Men of the Mercantile Marine who laid down their lives in maintaining the Services of Transport and Supply during the Great War ; and to those ranks and ratings of the Auxiliary vessels who sacrificed their lives in Home and Foreign waters so that the Merchant Fleet might keep the seas.

These are noble and memorable words ; and here let us note that they are but a sample of the phraseology of the Memorial inscriptions as a whole. They are unprovocative; there is no suggestion anywhere of exultation over a beaten foe. The word "Victory" is only once mentioned throughout the building, and the diction is as simple and stately as that of the Old Testament.

The rest of this bay, with the exception of the space occupied by the Cameron and Argyll Memorials, is almost entirely devoted to the Women's Services. There is a memorial bronze to Women beneath that of the Merchant Service, and another opposite, on the west wall, beneath the Women's Window. What a field of action they cover, and what memories they recall—of selfless devotion; of life and health risked in dangerous and exacting trades; of uncongenial, unheroic duties uncomplainingly performed; of aid and comfort rendered to wounded and dying in three continents. The crests of the various units concerned are depicted on the east wall; below comes an inscription which fittingly balances that of the Mercantile Marine above :—

In honour of all Scotswomen who, amid the stress of War, sought by their labours,

*sympathy and prayers, to obtain for their
country the blessings of Peace.*

Again no reference to triumph or victory.

Opposite, upon the western wall, are recorded the service and sacrifice of the Nursing
Services, by a bronze panel depicting stretcher-
bearers, nurses, and a wounded man, surmounted by the badges of the various nursing
units ; below, Laurence Binyon's familiar but
none the less lovely lines :—

"*They shall not grow old as we that are left
    grow old,
Age shall not weary them, nor the years con-
    demn,
At the going down of the sun and in the
    morning
We will remember them.*"

Appropriately included in this particular bay,
devoted mainly to the service and sacrifice of the
so-called Non-Combatants, upon the pier between the arches of the north side, is the
Memorial to the Chaplains to the Forces, of
whom no less than two hundred and seven gave

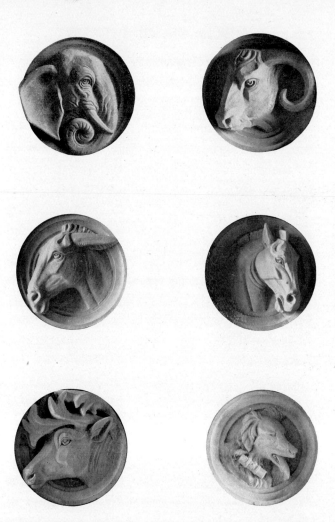

"REMEMBER ALSO THE HUMBLE BEASTS . . . . "

their lives on various fronts.[1]   It offers a re-
markably faithful representation of a Field Com-
munion Service, with its devastated landscape,
improvised Table (of ammunition cases) and
kneeling men.

Two unusual monuments, one of which has
already been mentioned, round off the contents
of this bay.   The first is a little panel on the
base of a pillar, dedicated to the Canaries and
Mice ; the other a frieze of the heads of various
transport animals employed by us in the War ;
a horse, a mule, a camel, and a reindeer, sub-
scribed with a passage adapted from the
Liturgy of the Greek Church :—" *Remember
also the Humble Beasts that served and died.*"
Perhaps in the place where Humble Beasts go
when they have completed their service, that
epitaph is recorded with modest pride.

Now we are back in the main Hall again.   The
Air Service Memorial on the west wall to our
left we have already examined.   The north wall,

---

[1] This is the *total* number.   Ten of these were attached to
Scottish units, but others were serving with English and
Dominion troops.

running the whole length of the Hall, is entirely occupied by Regimental Memorials, broken only by the archway into the Shrine. We will proceed therefore to the south-east bay, merely noting, as we pass the Shrine arch, the shields of the five great cities of Scotland—Aberdeen, Glasgow, Edinburgh, Dundee, and Perth, upheld by Angels disposed round the arch itself.

The south-east bay is devoted mainly to the other great fighting arms of the service, as distinct from the Infantry of the Line.

First, beneath the window depicting the Mechanism of War, we have the Memorial to the Royal Artillery, a bronze in relief, surmounted by their crest and motto " Ubique "—a motto gratefully remembered by many a hard-pressed and temporarily isolated infantry unit. The bronze itself depicts an eight-inch howitzer in action, a notably magnificent piece of work in this treasure-house of magnificence. Observe the amazingly life-like attitude of the men serving the gun—four of them ramming home the shell, while a fifth stands by with the cartridge. Artillery seems to inspire artists to their best

THE CANARIES AND MICE
(See p. 123)

work—witness Jagger's majestic composition at Hyde Park Corner in London.

Round this bronze are grouped the badges of the Machine Gun Corps, the Tank Corps, and other units whose service is not commemorated elsewhere.

And we may here note the care which has been taken by the designers of the Memorial that no act of service shall go unrecorded. In this very bay, on the pillar between the Memorials of the Gordons and the Greys, you may note a bronze panel inscribed as follows :—

In Memory of the Scottish Officers, Non-Commissioned Officers, and Men of the Household Cavalry who fell in the Great War, 1914-1918.

And elsewhere throughout the building, you will find :—

To Scotsmen of All Ranks who fell while serving in English, Irish, and Welsh Regiments, 1914-1918.

To Scotsmen of All Ranks who fell while serving with units of the British Dominions and Colonies, 1914-1918.

To the Memory of the Officers and Other Ranks of Scottish descent who fell while serving with the Indian Army during the Great War, 1914-1918.

Each of these panels is surmounted by an historical trophy of Scottish or other arms, in bronze, gold, and silver.

The southern wall of the bay is occupied by two Regimental Memorials, those of the Gordons and the Royal Scots Greys, already described. The west wall is adorned by a really beautiful and astonishingly ingenious composite trophy carved and tinted in stone, of the arms and equipment employed by the seven Scottish Yeomanry regiments during the War—the Fife and Forfar Yeomanry, the Lothians and Border Horse, the Scottish Horse, the Lovat Scouts, the Queen's Own Royal Glasgow Yeomanry, the Lanarkshire Yeomanry, and the Ayrshire Yeomanry. Everything is there—sabres and carbines, Lewis and Hotchkiss guns, bits and bridles, stirrups and holsters, bandoliers and pouches, bugles and pipes—all most skilfully and decoratively grouped, together with the appropriate guidons and lances. Note particularly the shield above, with the device of the broken spur, adopted in humorous resignation by those Yeomanry units which were dismounted to form the Seventy-Fourth Infantry Division in Palestine.

Below, in a row, are three more Memorial bronzes. That in the centre commemorates the work of that great Corps, the Royal Engineers, whose tradition it is that, though precluded as a rule from any form of self-defence, they must never allow the action of the enemy to interfere with the performance of their duty. Which of us who has seen them repairing a bridge, or constructing an emplacement, or restoring a broken field-telephone wire amid bursts of shrapnel, will ever forget their cool detachment and magnificent unconcern ? *Quo Fas et Gloria ducunt*, indeed. In the panel here you will see them at work upon some of their familiar tasks ; a detachment are throwing a bridge across a river, while Signallers send a Morse message ticking through space.

To right and left are the Memorial bronzes of

two other great and deservedly " Royal " Corps, the Royal Army Medical Corps, and the Royal Army Service Corps. The inscriptions are admirable in form and diction, as everywhere.

To the Officers and Men of the Royal Army Service Corps, who in their labours on every front, gave their lives to maintain our Armies in the field, 1914-1918

and

In Honour of All Ranks of the Royal Army Medical Corps, who combatting sickness, pain, and death, laid down their lives in the service of their fellow-men, 1914-1918.

And now we have nearly completed our tale of service. But not quite. On the pier between the arches leading out of the bay are four Memorials to those sturdy and characteristically independent organizations, the Scottish battalions of certain English territorial units—the London Scottish, the Liverpool Scottish, the Tyneside Scottish, and in a slightly different category, the South African Scottish.

The London Scottish were raised in 1859. Their first experience of active service was in the

South African War. In the Great War they grew to three battalions, and served on the Western Front (where they did exceptionally fine work at Messines in the difficult days of 1914), Macedonia, and Palestine. Seventy-five Officers and one thousand four hundred and sixty-eight Other Ranks gave their lives.

The Liverpool Scottish were raised in 1900, for service in the South African War. In the Great War they mustered three battalions, and worthily upheld the historic reputation of the King's Liverpool Regiment, to which they are affiliated.

The Tyneside Scottish formed the Twentieth, Twenty-second, Twenty-third, and Twenty-fourth Battalions of the famous Northumberland Fusiliers, or Fighting Fifth. They were raised in four weeks in 1914, and served with great distinction upon the Western Front. One hundred and eighteen Officers and two thousand five hundred and forty-two Other Ranks gave their lives.

The South African Scottish consisted of the Transvaal Scottish and Capetown Highlanders, but contained many men of the Boer blood and tradition—a source of natural pride to ourselves, and of astonishment to the enemy.   They were raised for service in the Great War against the German Colony of South West Africa—the first campaign in the whole War to be victoriously concluded.   Thereafter they were transferred to the Western Front, where room was found for them in a famous Scottish Division—the Ninth. They won undying fame at the First Battle of the Somme, in the costly but victorious struggle for Longueval and Delville Wood.   The South African War Memorial stands in Delville Wood to-day.

In the panel which jointly commemorates the service of these four units we see a soldier standing by a Scotsman's grave—with the familiar rough wooden cross, surmounted by a tattered " bunnet " and inscribed :—*Known only to God*. Above are the appropriate weapons—the targe, the broadsword, and dirk, with a Gaelic inscription which being interpreted means—" My Country, my Honour, and my God ".

Lastly, above the arch, we note a continua-

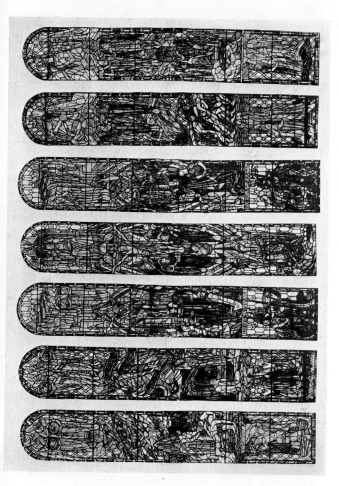

THE WINDOWS OF THE SHRINE

(These photographs will repay examination through a magnifying glass)

tion of the frieze of animal heads from the west bay ; a dog, an ox, an elephant, and a carrier pigeon, and a repetition of the inscription to the Humble Beasts.

So ends the rich record of material service and historic incident. But before we enter the Shrine, where things Temporal yield place to things Spiritual, let us pause outside this bay and contemplate, at the base of the pier between the arches, almost exactly opposite the King's Own Scottish Borderers Memorial, one of the latest additions to the Hall of Honour—a bronze medallion of Lord Haig, added since his death in 1928, barely six months after his own participation in the Dedication.

Lord Haig's are the only individual name and features delineated upon the walls of the Memorial. All Scotland will acclaim that distinction. Besides commanding the greatest force ever put into the field in the history of our country, Douglas Haig was himself the living embodiment of the highest type of soldier. He might have figured in the pages of Bunyan. He possessed two outstanding characteristics. In the first place he was always the same—equally cool and unruffled in good times or in bad ; and his quality was such that he invariably imparted a measure of his own great spirit to the men who followed him.   In the second, he realized the debt and deference due from a commander to the brave men who have won his victories for him.   That is why, whenever he spoke for the Army, and particularly when he had to return thanks for some distinction conferred upon himself, he invariably referred the credit to All Ranks—and All Ranks loved him for it.   That is why this medallion is inscribed, quite simply :— Haig, 1861-1928.   Nothing more was necessary.

THE CHAPLAIN'S MEMORIAL
(See p. 122)

CHAPTER VIII

THE SHRINE

STAND once more within the main doorway of the building under the figure of *Réveillé*, and look across the Hall of Honour. You will see before you an immensely lofty stone arch, the upper part of which frames the figure of St Michael, Captain of the Heavenly Host, and of those earthly hosts which fight in a just cause. He hangs from the roof of the Shrine, folded in his own wings and silhouetted against the windows behind him. His face, unlike that of the majestic figure representing the Survival of the Spirit which broods over the outer entrance, is plainly visible, and at noon on a sunny day is brightly illuminated from a little window set specially for the purpose high up in the southern wall of the Shrine.

The lower part of the arch is guarded by gates of wrought iron. They are open: let us enter.

It will be useless to suggest a methodical tour

of inspection here. Eyes and feet turn instinctively to the central feature of the Shrine—the heart and core of the whole Memorial—the Stone of Remembrance, and the Casket.

The Stone is set upon an outcrop of the Rock itself, which here breaks through the flagged pavement as if eager to shoulder its just burden. No attempt has been made to dress it or modify its contours, but already its surface has been worn smooth and glistening by the feet of the pilgrims.

Upon the face of the Stone, which is of green Corona marble, is cut the Cross of Sacrifice, surmounted by the inscription, *Their Name Liveth*. On the top, guarded by kneeling Angels, like the Ark of the Covenant itself, stands the shining Casket, of cunningly wrought steel—the gift of the King and Queen. It contains the Rolls of Honour which bear the names of Scotland's dead, deposited for the rest of time in the ineffable peace of this mystic, enchanted spot.

As a mere work of art the Casket will fascinate you. Observe the beautiful workmanship of the

THE ENTRANCE TO THE SHRINE

lock and hinges ; the figures of the Angels holding shields, upon which are emblazoned the
Virtues—of St Margaret of Scotland—of St
Andrew—all nobly designed and exquisitely
wrought. Still, the appeal of outward beauty
must here take second place : it is what lies
within that matters. Nearly everybody in Scotland has a proprietary interest in the contents of
that Casket.

Let us next look up at the windows, whose
lovely colouring is mainly responsible for the atmosphere of quiet peace. They are of deeper
hue than those of the Hall of Honour—rich
blues, greens, and purples. They tell, in symbol
and allegory, the History of Strife—its origin, its
rise, its fall, and its final overthrow by the Power
of the Spirit.

There are seven of these windows. At the
top of the first pair, on the left, you will see the
Creation of the World, proceeding from day
to day according to Biblical story—Light and
Darkness, The Firmament, Earth and Sea, Sun
and Moon. Various Signs of the Zodiac are set
beneath.

The general theme of these two windows is the Birth of War. We see the coming of Strife to the world. Abel lies dead, the first to die in the history of Man. Eve, eternal type of solicitous Motherhood, supports her son's head upon her knees. Adam stands by, in tragic foreboding. In the background, ruthless but sorrowful, we see the Avenger ; behind him, the Tree of Knowledge. *Dust thou art and to dust thou shalt return*, is the dread sentence which he pronounces. Turning to the second window close by, we see, crouching upon a river bank, the fugitive figure of the exiled Cain, haunted by the hosts of Evil, on horse and foot. *Thy brother's blood crieth unto me from the ground*, is ringing in his ears.

But even Strife can evoke certain complementary virtues. At the base of the first window is a panel depicting Faith, typified by the story of Abraham and Isaac : below the second we behold the genesis of Law and Order —Moses with the Ark of the Covenant.

Turn now to the opposite side of the Shrine, or here you will find the answer of the New

Testament to the Old. Here are depicted the decline of Strife and the overthrow of Tyranny. Conspicuous are two delineations of the enslavement of Man—one, the figure of Ruthlessness enthroned; the other, Mankind harnessed to a battering ram. *How long, O Lord, holy and true, dost thou not avenge our blood on them that dwell on the earth?*

That appeal is soon answered: in the adjacent window we behold the souls of the righteous soaring upward, and read:—*And they overcame him by the blood of the Lamb, and they loved not their lives unto the death.* Above both scenes hover Angels, with the vials of wrath; above these are the four Horsemen of the Revelation, who follow the Rider on the White Horse, whose face is set toward the Throne.

There remain the three windows at the end of the Shrine, facing towards the Hall of Honour. That in the centre utters the final word of joy and ecstasy—the Spirit Triumphant. At the summit stands the Eternal, with the Dove fluttering above His head and the Lamb resting at His feet. Below is the Cross of the Crucifixion, which through all history has symbolized the path to Triumph by the way of Sacrifice. Take particular note of the figure itself : it is not nailed to the Cross ; it is free. No longer does its posture represent Suffering and Death, but Resurrection and Ascension.

Round the Cross are grouped the four Elements. At its foot, for the third time in this our pilgrimage, we see the Pelican, the symbol of mother-love.

Below all we behold Peace enthroned, supported by the East and the West, with the dead figure of War at her feet. A wounded soldier lies gazing hopefully upward.

The two flanking windows implement the general theme. Their message might be summed up in the text, *All Thy works do praise Thee, O Lord ;* for here we see Man, freed from the burdens of War, devoting himself anew to the activities of Peace. The window on the left shows us a Shepherd, a Reaper, and a Kneeling Warrior, about to convert his sword into a ploughshare. Philosophy and Music grace the scene, with Hope and Courage typified above.

ST. MICHAEL

(See p. 133)

At the peak of the window the Elders, with their eyes set in the direction of the centre scene, are casting down their crowns before the Spirit.

In the panel at the foot are presented two defenders of Scottish freedom—Galgacus, who opposed the Romans, and William Wallace.

The theme is maintained and perfected in the window on the right. Here you may see Craftsmen and Men of Science at their task. Justice and Patience attend their labours. Wisdom, in the form of Age, instructs Youth—a child gazing hopefully into the future. Below, Alexander III and Robert the Bruce stand shoulder to shoulder with a modern kilted soldier.

Such is the message, the message of Hope and Deliverance, presented by these

> —storied windows richly dight,
> Casting a dim religious light.

Before examining the other outstanding feature of the Shrine, let us turn towards the entrance, and observe the inner side of the tall arch. It is encircled by the Tree of Empire, supporting upon its branches the shields of India, the Union of South Africa, Australia, the Royal Arms of Scotland, Newfoundland, New Zealand, and Canada.

THE FRIEZE

Below the windows, right round the interior of the Shrine, runs a boldly executed frieze of bronze—bronze which looks like gold—depicting one hundred typical figures of the War, and including at least one representative of every rank and unit employed. Every weapon, every variety of uniform, and every article of equipment used is here included, reproduced in faithful and unerring detail. The figures follow one another in close procession, against a martial background of guns and limbers, of ambulances, of tanks and aeroplanes. They all face north : in other words, there are two processions, converging upon the far end of the Shrine, where behind the Casket a bronze panel, set below the centre window, displays two wreaths—of thorn and bay—Sacrifice and Victory—with the Sword of Honour between.

THE BRONZE FRIEZE

Starting on the left, the first figure which we overtake is that of a Cameron Highlander, with khaki kilt-apron, ankle puttees, steel helmet, and extra ammunition pouches. He is a type of early 1916 : he carries no elaborate anti-gas apparatus on his chest. Next comes a Royal Army Medical Corps group of four figures, including a surgeon in field operating kit. Ahead of these we see a soldier heavily clad in duffle, with a cowl over his head and snow-shoes on his feet : he represents the Russian Expeditionary Force, which suffered the rigours of Murmansk and Archangel. Before him strides an Army Chaplain, undistinguishable from the average officer save for his clerical badge and lack of weapons.

Next comes a Sapper of a Tunnelling Company—a burly, bare-armed figure, with his cap on the back of his head, carrying a pick. You may see his counterpart nowadays repairing Piccadilly, or laying a gas-main in Princes Street. He is preceded by a novel and unfamiliar type, a Tank-gunner, whose most conspicuous article of equipment is a mesh of chain mail over the face

—the one vulnerable spot behind a Tank loophole.

Now we come to a pair of Lewis Gunners of the Highland Light Infantry, one carrying the slim, portable gun, the other the disc-like leather cases which contain the revolving magazines. They are following a Gunner of a different type —a Field Artilleryman trudging by the head of the leading mule of an Ammunition limber. The going is evidently bad : the man's head, encased in a woollen helmet beneath a tin hat, after the ungraceful but comfortable fashion of those days, is bowed low ; that of his beast droops, too, in patient weariness. Just ahead march two privates of the King's Own Scottish Borderers, in Flanders winter kit. Their legs are wrapped in sandbags, their ground-sheets are spread over their shoulders and packs against the endless rain ; their rifle locks are carefully protected from the all-pervading mud by a wrapping of canvas. Note the profile of the man in the Balmoral bonnet—a Lowland Scot of the true Border breed. They are preceded by a mounted Signaller Corporal of the Royal Engineers, with his reel of telegraph wire on his back. He follows two privates of the Black Watch, wrapped up against the cold in woollen muffler and helmet. The procession is headed, so far as the first panel is concerned— there are two on either side of the Shrine—by a Lieutenant of the Royal Air Force, in over-alls and flying helmet, who stands beside his machine, map in hand.

The second panel begins, for us, with two Gunners, one of the Field, the other of the Horse Artillery. The first, a brawny, shirt-sleeved figure, carries an eighteen-pounder shell. The second is a driver, distinguished by his steel leg-guard, worn for protection against the pressure of the pole. Next come two more repre-sentatives of the Mounted Services—a trooper of the Lovat Scouts, in diced bonnet, and a Lance-Corporal of the Scots Greys. Then a Motor Transport Driver of the Royal Army Ser-vice Corps, in the grubby, fleece-lined leather coat of the Army chauffeur. These are preceded by the first representative of the Navy, a Midship-man : he looks strangely slim and trim in this world of plodding soldiers laden like pack-mules.

Now we come upon a piper—unexpectedly enough a New Zealander, of the Auckland Regiment, 16th Waikato Company. He wears a kilt-apron, like our own Jocks, but his glengarry is slightly different. Before him, on foot, tramps a trooper of the Lothians and Border Horse. Ahead of him, also on foot, strolls a British General, complete with the insignia of the British Officer on active service—a walking stick. The General's face is strangely familiar—as indeed are practically all the faces in the frieze to those who know them; for most of them are portraits. A Sergeant of the Scots Guards heads the procession.

We cross the end of the Shrine, between the Casket and the centre panel, to meet the other procession.

A piper of the Gordon Highlanders leads the way, followed by privates of the 16th Canadian Scottish and of the Argyll and Sutherland Highlanders. Next comes a Corporal of the Machine Gun Corps, followed by a sturdy figure in sea-

boots and jersey, spanner in hand : he is a Submarine Rating of the Royal Navy. Three of the
next four figures are Navy men too—a Lieutenant, a Petty Officer Gunner's Mate, and an
Able Seaman. The other figure is that of a
Second Lieutenant of the Royal Scots : note
that in faithful pursuance of the principle of dis-
playing every item of modern war equipment,
he has been given a Service revolver and a Mills
bomb to carry.

Now we come to the fifth and last panel.
First we encounter a Mechanic of the Royal
Flying Corps—an upstanding, curly-headed boy
in the dapper, high-buttoned, long-forgotten
tunic of the pre-Air Force days. Behind him
comes the first reminder of our Eastern campaigns—a private of the Royal Scots Fusiliers,
in sun helmet and khaki shorts. Note that on
his feet he wears wire sandals, for marching on
sand.

Another Naval series follows—an Able Seaman, Seaman Gunner ; a Private of the Royal
Marines ; a Warrant Officer of the Navy, in
heavy duffle coat and hood, such as were donned

K

against the wintry weather of the North Sea ; a
Stoker, dressed for fire-fighting purposes and
carrying a hose—his head is completely covered
except for nose and eyes—a Signalman, tele-
scope in hand ; after him another Stoker, a
more conventional figure this time, with shovel
and sweat rag ; then a Mine-sweeper in a woollen
nightcap, an obvious recruit from the lay world,
as his moustache indicates. Last in the contingent comes a Seaman of the Royal Naval
Volunteer Reserve, in lifejacket, carrying a coil
of rope.

Now we encounter another unfamiliar figure
—a trooper of the Scottish Horse attached to the
Imperial Camel Corps, in shorts and sun-helmet :
beside him is visible the bridling, mincing head
of his unaccustomed steed. Next come two
Seaforths, a Private and a Corporal, the one
equipped for the trenches of Flanders, the other
for the desert. They are followed by a Private
of the Scottish Rifles, also in tropical uniform.
Upon his heels follows a Captain of the Royal
Garrison Artillery, or Heavy Gunners ; then an
Army Service Corps Driver, booted and spurred,

and leading one of his horses. Upon his shoulder-straps you will observe the letters A.S.C. This detail is as meticulously correct as all the others : the title " Royal " was conferred at the end of the War.

Now comes another interesting figure, a Sergeant of the Royal Engineers with carrier pigeons, attended by a despatch-carrying dog. " The Humble Beasts ", we note, have not been forgotten here.

The last two men in the procession are Highlanders, privates of the London Scottish and South African Scottish respectively.

Finally, in their trim uniforms and workmanlike shoes, march representatives of the four great sister Services—Queen Mary's Auxiliary Army Corps (better and affectionately known under their original sobriquet of " The Waacs"), the Voluntary Aid Detachment, the Women's Royal Naval Service, and the Women's Royal Air Force. They come last in the procession ; but they are preceded by such an escort as few women ever had.

So ends this unforgettable record, almost life-

size in dimension and utterly lifelike in effect.
Above it, in letters of stone, running right round
the Shrine, is the inscription :—

*The souls of the righteous are in the hand of
God. There shall no evil happen to them.
They are in peace.*

Below, in letters of gold :—

*Others also there are who perished unknown.
Their sacrifice is not forgotten, and their
names, though lost to us, are written in the
Books of God.*

We have finished. We take a final survey of
the Shrine—of the Casket, the Windows, the
golden Procession, the smooth-worn Rock itself.
Then we pass out through the tall arch, into the
Hall of Honour. We take a backward look at
St Michael, framed in the arch and illuminated
now by a ray of the noonday sun ; then a forward
and final glance at the glorious figure of *Réveillé*
over the doorway. Next moment we are out
in Crown Square again, and our Pilgrimage is
ended.

RÉVEILLÉ
(See p. 118)

CHAPTER IX

NE OBLIVISCARIS

ABOVE, you will see the Latin motto of a famous Highland regiment. It can be translated into equally good Scots—" Dinna Forget ! "

It is quoted here because at times we have to remind ourselves of certain things. Not long ago a group of permanently disabled soldiers, who have been quartered for ten long years in a Military Hostel just outside London, and seem likely, alas, to spend the rest of their broken lives there, proffered a petition to the Hospital authorities, praying that when they took their brief and laborious walks abroad they might be permitted to wear some kind of civilian dress in place of the usual hospital blue—that once familiar uniform, with its white facings and natty red tie. Asked for their reasons, they explained that more than once passers-by, usually young people, had mistaken them for inmates of the local poorhouse.

Here is a parable capable of application to a larger theme.

" Usually young people." That is the disturbing part of it. The New Generation does not seem to know, or at least, to care.

As for caring or not caring, that is their own business. And let us admit at once that those who decline to care have a definite and not unreasonable case. They say, in effect, to the Old Generation :

"Seventeen years ago, you involved our country in a War. That War did not end until civilization had been shattered, and our expectation of (and right to) a life of normality had been shattered with it. You say that you won that War, but the results are not apparent. You spent eight thousand million pounds, upon which we are paying the interest ; you produced an industrial condition under which two million people are out of employment ; you created a state of unrest throughout our hitherto acquiescent Empire which has loosened all ties, and in some directions threatens complete disruption. Having accomplished this, you have handed over to us the broken fragments of the World which should have been ours, and bidden us piece them together again. We are doing the best we can, but we are not enjoying the task, and you can hardly expect us to feel grateful or respectful to the people who rendered it necessary. Above all, you must not expect us to share the feeling of sentimental satisfaction with which you appear to look back upon your own performance. You say that those were great and inspiring days in the history of our Nation—days to be remembered with pride and thanksgiving. But we know better. The veil of sentiment has been torn aside : the real truth is beginning to come out."

Then they quote to you various passages from one of the new style War novels.

To engage in debate upon this matter in these pages would be both unprofitable and unseemly. But there is one thing which we are entitled to point out. We are at present far too close to that world tragedy, the Great War, to be able to judge it in any true perspective. It is too soon to decide whether we were right or wrong to take up arms at all ; or whether we could have evaded that responsibility had we wished to do so ; or whether we are or are not the saner and sounder as a nation for having passed through the furnace.   History must settle that for us, for we are quite incapable of settling it for ourselves.   All we can do at present is to react (and reacting we undoubtedly are) to a series of nation-wide emotions, most of them conflicting and all of them extreme.   We have been reacting for sixteen years, and the end is not yet in sight, so tremendous was the backwash of that awful conflict.

We began by being carried away, as men have been carried away throughout the ages, by the fever of War.   Everybody had but one ambition —to be in the movement in some capacity. Young men enlisted for War service, young women registered for some service ancillary to the War.   Older people freely offered themselves and their resources to the cause, according to their means and ability.   The springs of charity were opened wide.   War Relief Societies sprang up everywhere, to aid the sick, the wounded, the lonely. Half the great mansions in England and Scotland became private hospitals. For the moment public opinion was absolutely solid. Rich and poor were brothers, and said so.

Mid-channel, and the mood had changed. The first fine enthusiasm had gone; there was weariness and industrial fatigue; recrimination. But teeth were set: this was going to be a fight to a finish.

At last came Victory, resounding and complete; exultation; and blind determination to make a hero of everybody who had contributed thereto.

Then followed one vast reaction. Everybody announced that the War must now be forgotten. We had to get back to business. War books were unsaleable, War topics taboo. Having talked about nothing but the War for five years, we decided never to talk about it again.

And now, twelve years later, we are talking about it more than ever. But the note is different. War has become a monstrous, unspeakable thing, and all the nations of Christendom are to-day combined in earnest, eager debate to drive it for ever from among men.   So far, so good.

But, as always happens, we cannot stop.   Our mood is veering again, this time in a particularly perilous direction.   A great deal of the opprobrium which belongs to war is being transferred to the soldier.   To-day in certain eyes the soldier is no longer a hero, or for that matter, a man.   He is variously depicted as a machine, a slave, or a dupe ; frequently as a brute or a coward.   And however he may bear himself, or have borne himself, in the performance of his duty, no kind of credit must attach to his achievement, for to commend him would be to commend his trade.   That is the general tone of retrospective War literature to-day.   The institution and the instrument are equally condemned.

Plainly, then, our reactions and emotions upon the subject of recent history are at present too fluid to have any lasting value.   We must leave it to Time to crystallize them.   Meanwhile we can hardly blame the New Generation for not caring.

In any case, it behoves us to be very, very tender with the New Generation, for theirs has been a barren inheritance. They have been robbed of the most blessed possession of Youth —illusion—and they are facing sophistication before their time. They are confronted by problems which never troubled us, and they are handling them with a courage and originality which we never knew, for we never needed it. And they have to do this without any help, because a whole generation is missing in our world to-day—the vanished million who would have formed the natural bridge across the gulf that always lies between impatient youth and intolerant middle-age. The bridge is there, but most of its stoutest timbers are missing. Can we wonder that the New Generation are chary of crossing it ?

But when it comes to knowing, that is a different matter altogether. They *must* know, and especially they must know what manner of men those were, in the lump, to whose memory we have erected our War Memorials. If knowing comes, caring will follow as surely as day follows night. And to care will be to remember—and that is all that our dead ask of us.

But before we leave our hundred thousand sons and brothers to their honoured rest, one or two last reflections may not be amiss.

In the first place, in the second place, and in the third place, was their sacrifice in vain? Were their lives wholly wasted? That is the dread which lies always at the bottom of every heart. To-day, as we are sadly aware, there is no lack of voices to proclaim that the sacrifice *was* vain and the lives utterly thrown away. Again, only Time can show.

But whatever the final verdict may be, that vanished generation have left behind them something which neither Time can efface nor Posterity belittle—something *aere perennius*—two unforgettable lessons. The first is that Man can always rise superior to his surroundings—surroundings which, viewed in retrospect and in cold blood, appear humanly insupportable—as a thousand tales of unshaken fortitude and un-

canny cheerfulness (flippancy, if you like)
remind us. The second, more trite but none
the less true, is that a community is never so
united, never so mutually helpful, never so full
of simple Christian decency, as when it is facing
a common danger and striving for what it regards
as a common ideal. Men who died to reaffirm
such truths as these can never wholly be said
to have died in vain.

And herein seems to lie the true lesson, the
true inspiration, of our national War Memorials.
We do not need to be versed in history or
biography to grasp their message. We can hear
it in our own ears as we stand within the Shrine
upon the summit of the Castle Rock—a message
of hope for our world, our floundering, dis-
illusioned world, to-day.

Fortitude as a people we possess, and always
did ; but we lack vision—perspective—above
all, confidence. We are prepared to stay the
course, but we are never sanguine about winning
the race. We are haunted to-day by two
spectres, Distress and Distrust. We are dis-
couraged about ourselves, and deeply suspicious

of one another, man and man, class and class. But the men to whom we raised the Cenotaph, the man who lies in the Abbey, the men whose names are recorded within the Casket on the Rock, were neither despondent nor suspicious. Their sturdy confidence and their humorous philosophy were the wonder of friend and foe, while in matters of mutual reliance they were as brothers.

Here then seems to be the talisman for which we are groping. Its name is Duty—the simple duty of living up to the tradition in which these men died, and of fulfilling the trust which they have plainly bequeathed to us. Let us see to it that we do not fail them, for they never failed us.

APPENDIX

SOME two hundred Artists, Craftsmen, and Labourers were responsible for the actual execution of the work connected with the Memorial. They were directed from first to last by the Architect, Sir Robert Lorimer, A.R.A., who died September 13th, 1929. He passed away before his time, to the deep sorrow of his many friends, but his great conception had been carried out, and the Memorial stood, finished and proved, upon the Castle Rock.

The following is a list of those variously responsible for the execution of the work :—

PHYLLIS BONE.
> *Exterior*— Unicorn and Lion at Entrance.
> Capitals of Niches and Gargoyles.
> Bronze handles of Entrance Doors.
> *Interior*— Eight Roundels, containing Heads of Animals that served.
> Panel with Canaries and Mice.

ALEX. CARRICK, A.R.S.A.
> *Exterior*— Figures of Justice and Courage, south elevation.
> *Interior*— Bronze Panels to R.A. and R.E. in south-east bay.

C. d'O. Pilkington Jackson.

Exterior—	Badges of the Services.
	Divisional Signs.
	Royal Lion (over Porch).
Interior—	Figure of Réveillé over the entrance to the Hall of Honour.
	Bosses in Roof of Porch.
	Inner and outer faces of Arch leading to Shrine.
	Navy, Air Force, Royal Marine, Mercantile Marine, Household Cavalry, Indian, English, Irish, and Welsh ; Colonial and Dominions ; and Yeomanry Memorials.
	All Service Badges.
	All lettering in stone and bronze.
	Keystones over the windows.
	Modelling, Bronze Work and Carving in connection with all Regimental Memorials.
	Medallion to Earl Haig.

Hazel Kennedy. Bronze Panel in memory of Chaplains.

Percy Portsmouth, R.S.A.

Figure above Entrance Door (Exterior) representing " Survival of the Spirit ".

Figures of Freedom and Charity in exterior niches.

George Salvesen.

Exterior— Figures of Peace and Mercy, south elevation.

Interior— Modelling Planets above windows in Shrine.

Douglas Strachan, LL.D., H.R.S.A.

The whole of the Stained Glass.

Designs for Planets above windows in Shrine.

John R. Sutherland (Hon. Heraldic Artist to the Lyon Court).

All Heraldic Drawings for Exterior and Interior, in consultation with the Lyon King and F. J. Grant, Lyon Clerk.

Alice Meredith-Williams.

Exterior— Group at apex of Shrine, " Calling of St Andrew ".

Group of Angels on buttresses of Shrine.

Figures of Truth and Knowledge.

Interior— Figure of St Michael in Shrine.

Four Angels on corners of Stone of Remembrance.

Figures of Steel Casket.

Bronze Panels to the Women's Services and Nursing Services in south-west bay.

Modelling of Bronze Frieze in Shrine.

ALICE MEREDITH-WILLIAMS—*continued*.
>　*Interior*— Modelling of Memorial to London, Liverpool, South African, and Tyneside Scottish in east bay.
>　Modelling of Pelican in Porch.

MORRIS MEREDITH-WILLIAMS.
>　Designs and Cartoons for Bronze Frieze in Shrine, for London Scottish Memorial, and for Pelican in Porch.

THOMAS HADDEN.　Ironwork of Screen leading into Shrine, and Steel Casket. Ironwork of Doors.

W. & A. CLOW.　Wood Carving of St Michael. Figure, Doors, etc.

NEIL M'LEOD & SONS LTD.
>　Builders.　Foreman—John Archibald.

NATHANIEL GRIEVE.
CHARLES HENSHAW.　　} Woodwork.
M'DONALD & CRESWICK.

SINGER & CO.　Bronze Foundry.

ALLAN & SONS.　Stone of Remembrance. Granite Floor.

THOMAS BEATTIE.　Stone Capitals of Columns and Shields of Counties.

DONALDSON & BURNS.
>　Stone Carvers for Phyllis Bone and A. Meredith-Williams.

W. Miles Johnston.
> Heraldic Blazoning and Painting.

A. C. Wood & Son. Painter Work, Gilding, etc.

George Waterston & Sons Ltd.
> Bookbinding.

David Reid & Gibson.   Quantity Surveyors

John Cordiner.   Clerk of Works.

HAUNTING EDINBURGH

By

FLORA GRIERSON

With 16 Illustrations in Colour and 6 Pencil Drawings by KATHERINE CAMERON, A.R.E., R.S.W., and 8 Reproductions of Title-pages of old Scottish books.

Large Royal 8vo.   20s. net.

Also a Special Edition on hand-made paper, limited to 100 numbered copies, each copy signed by the author and containing an etching specially done for this edition signed by the artist. £2 2s. net. (out of print).

" Of the many books recently issued on Edinburgh Miss Flora Grierson's holds a very high—perhaps even the highest place.   She tempers her appreciation with a discerning criticism admirably expressed . . . the chapter on ' Edinburgh to-day ' is simply first-rate . . . for the Scot this book will make a superb New Year's present."
Spectator.

" Miss Grierson's book weaves past and present so evenly and cunningly together, that one who has never set eyes on the city can read the book with excitement and pleasure."—*Fortnightly Review.*

" A vivid, elastic narrative, and out of the mass of picturesque detail emerges a clear outline of the city's story, a vivid human story, full of curious lore and related with frequent wit and humour."—*Observer.*

JOHN LANE THE BODLEY HEAD LTD., VIGO ST., W.1

THE BOOK OF
THE CLYDE

By

DONALD MAXWELL

Illustrated in Line and Colour by the Author
Demy 8vo.   1os. 6d. net.

" A charming series of drawings and writings of the
river from its source to the Firth.   Mr. Maxwell, with
pen or pencil, moves brightly along the changing landscape."—*Times.*

" Mr. Maxwell makes a pleasant book of the river's
pilgrimage, catching its lore with a cheerful pen and its
landscape with an able pencil."—*Manchester Guardian.*

" Mr. Maxwell catches the spirit of Clydeside both in
his drawings and in his impressions, and anybody who
thinks of going there will find his book a good equipment."—*Daily Telegraph.*

" Mr. Maxwell writes discursively and engagingly of
the scenery in a style always familiar and frequently
graced by a fine allusiveness.   The drawings are exceed-
ingly beautiful."—*Scotsman.*

" Humorous, urbane, and observant.   Mr. Maxwell
wanders up the Clyde, a pilgrim with a pencil, drawing
delicate sketches, making amusing and penetrating
comment."—*T.P.'s Weekly.*

JOHN LANE THE BODLEY HEAD LTD., VIGO ST., W.1

FAIR PERTHSHIRE

By

HAMISH MILES

Illustrated in Colour and Black and White

by John McGhie

15s. net.

" Mr. Miles makes a very agreeable guide to this land of varied charms.   He has assembled an attractive budget of description, history and legend, and in its illustration he has found an accomplished colleague in Mr. McGhie."—*Scotsman*.

" A handsome volume by that popular annalist of Scottish beauty, Hamish Miles, illustrated charmingly by John McGhie.   This is delightful all through."—*Evening Standard*.

" Any one who has not yet explored that delectable Scottish county, but wishes to do so, could take no better cicerone with him to guide him in explorations than his admirable and attractive book.   The literary quality of the work is high and the narrative manner bright and interesting."—*Truth*.

JOHN LANE THE BODLEY HEAD LTD., VIGO ST., W.1

STEINHAUER

The Kaiser's Master Spy

Edited by S. T. FELSTEAD. With an Introduction by Admiral Sir REGINALD HALL, K.C.M.G., formerly Director of Naval Intelligence. With 25 illustrations. 18s. net.

Steinhauer was the guiding spirit in German Espionage from 1900 to 1914. He here describes his visit to England in July 1914, one month before the outbreak of War, and has many stories to tell of famous spies of various nationalities with whom he came in contact between 1900 and 1914, which are more exciting than most fiction. He also gives his own personal impressions of the Emperor, with whom he served first as an officer on the " Hohenzollern " and then as bodyguard for many years.

" I welcome this book, which will give to the public, the discerning public, a picture of the Spy as he really is . . . an amazing essay in self-revelation."
HAROLD NICOLSON in the *Evening Standard*.

" Steinhauer has told his own story in a remarkable work."—*Daily Mail*.

JOHN LANE THE BODLEY HEAD LTD., VIGO ST., W.1